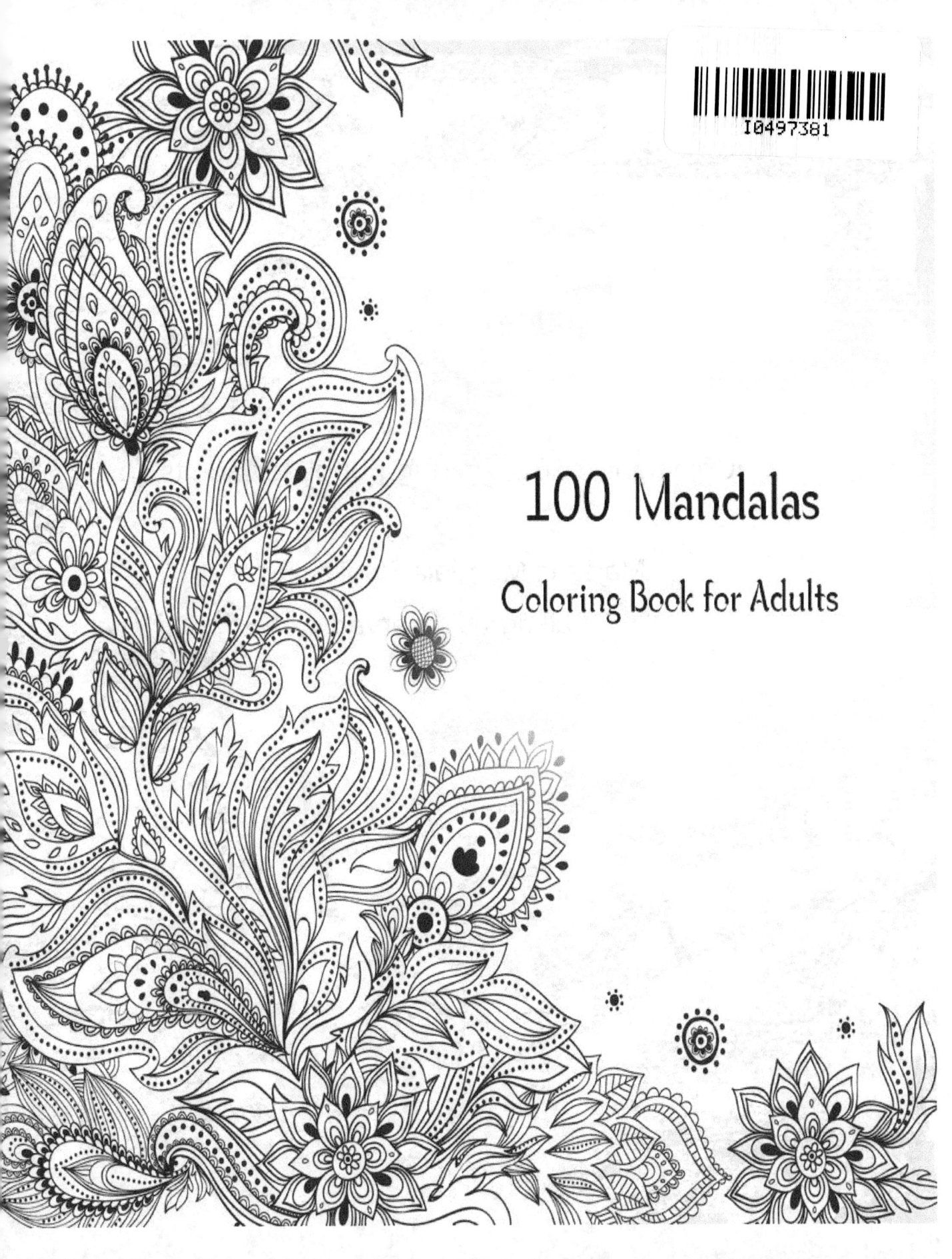

Copyright © 2020, coloring book for adults

by

Majestic Mandala Publishing

all rights reserved.

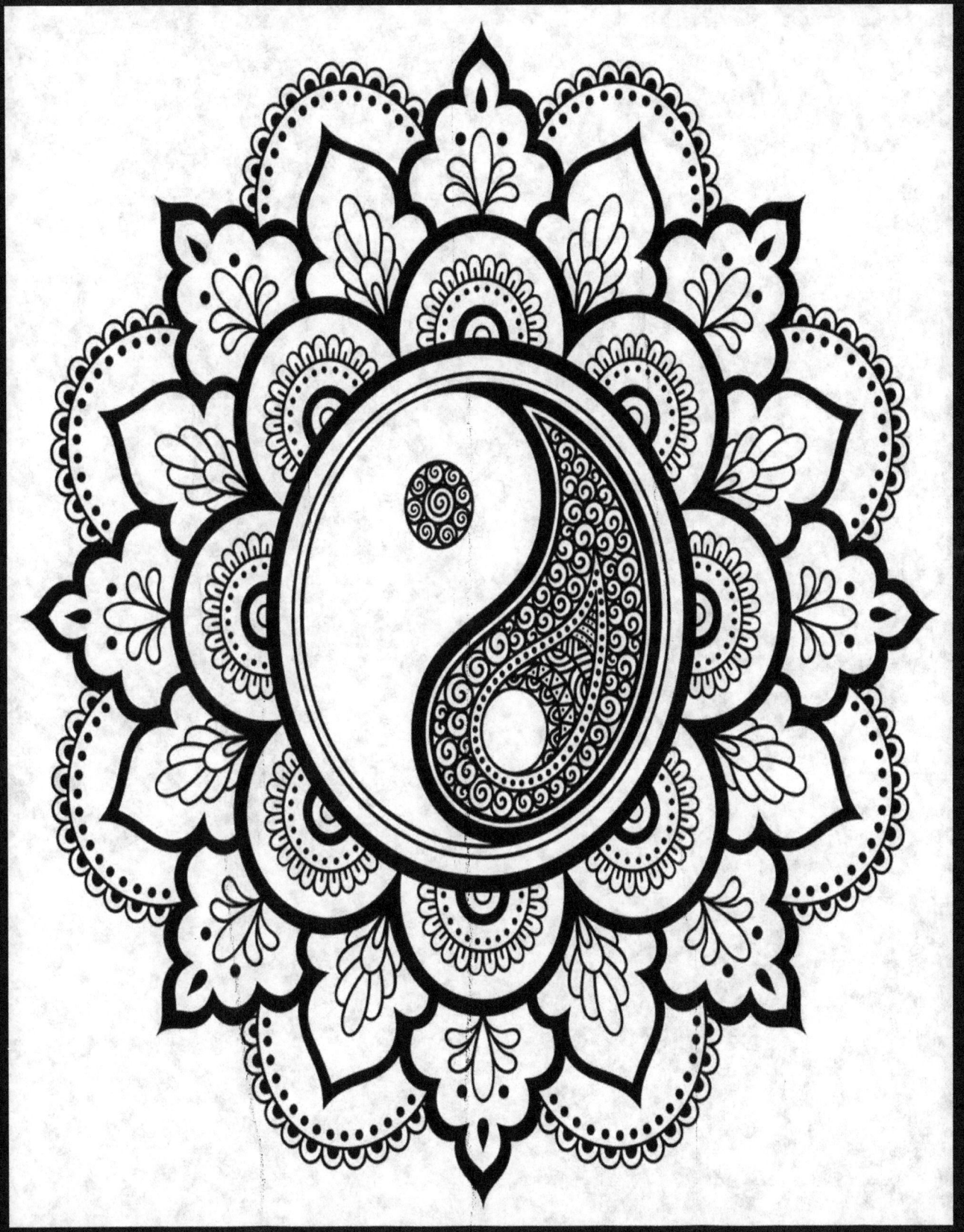

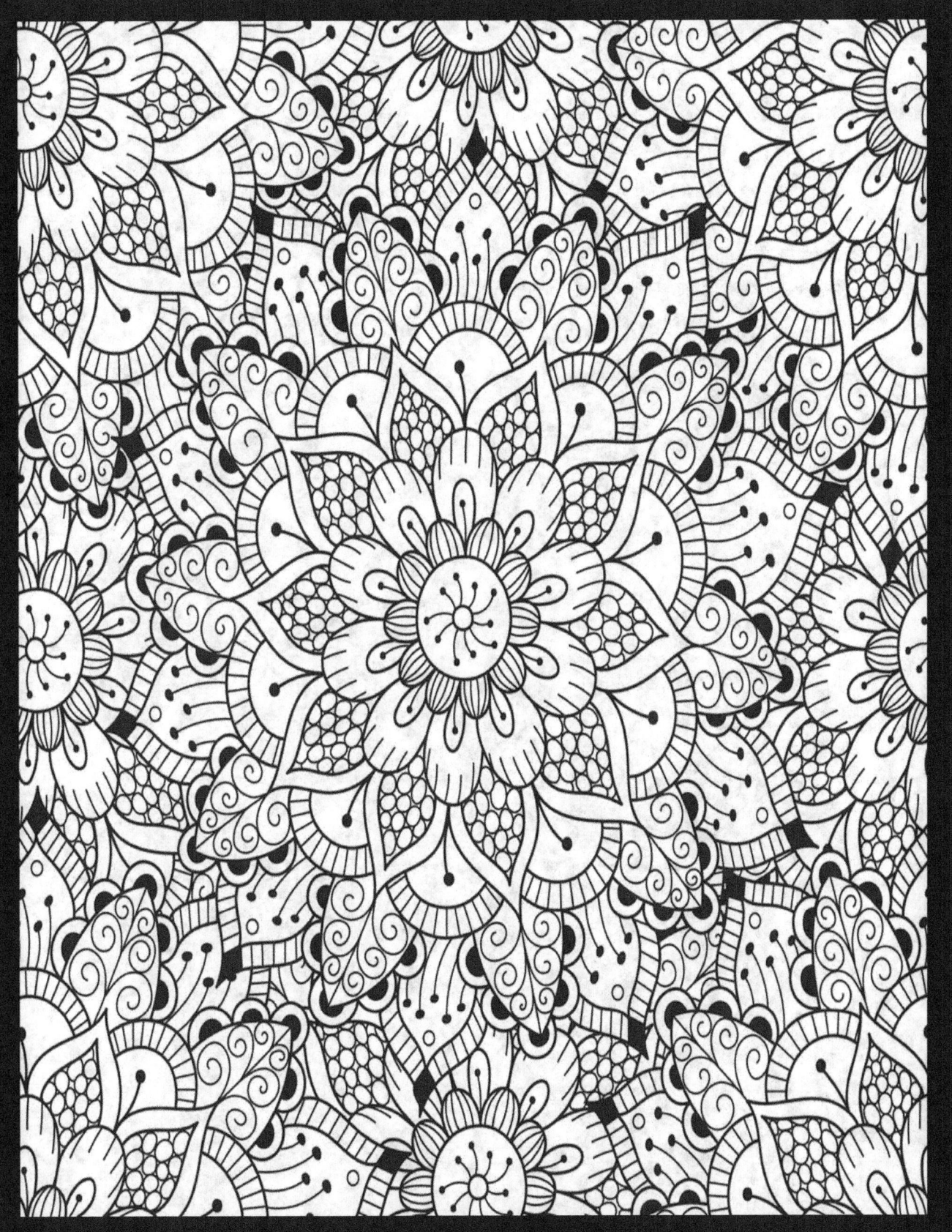

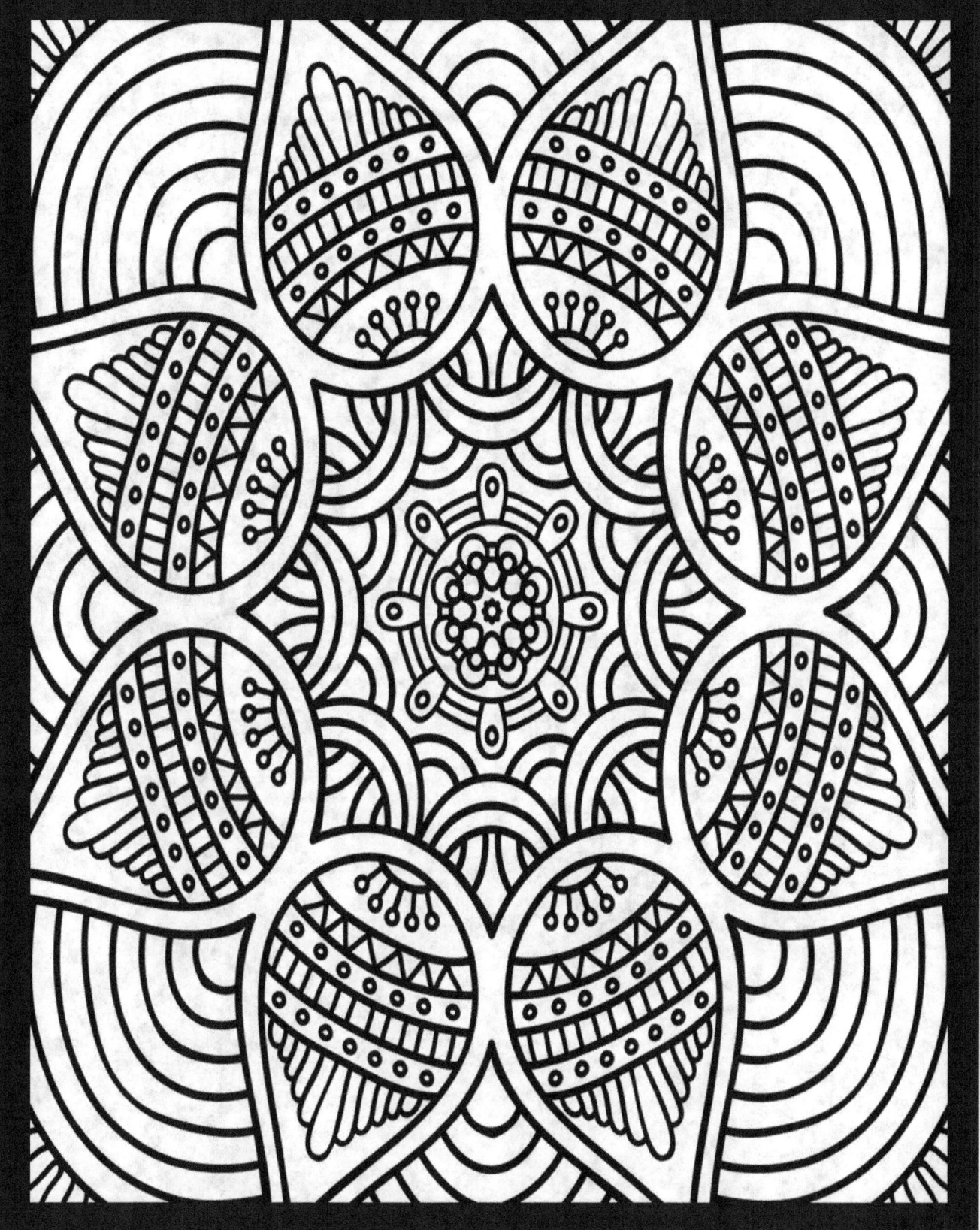

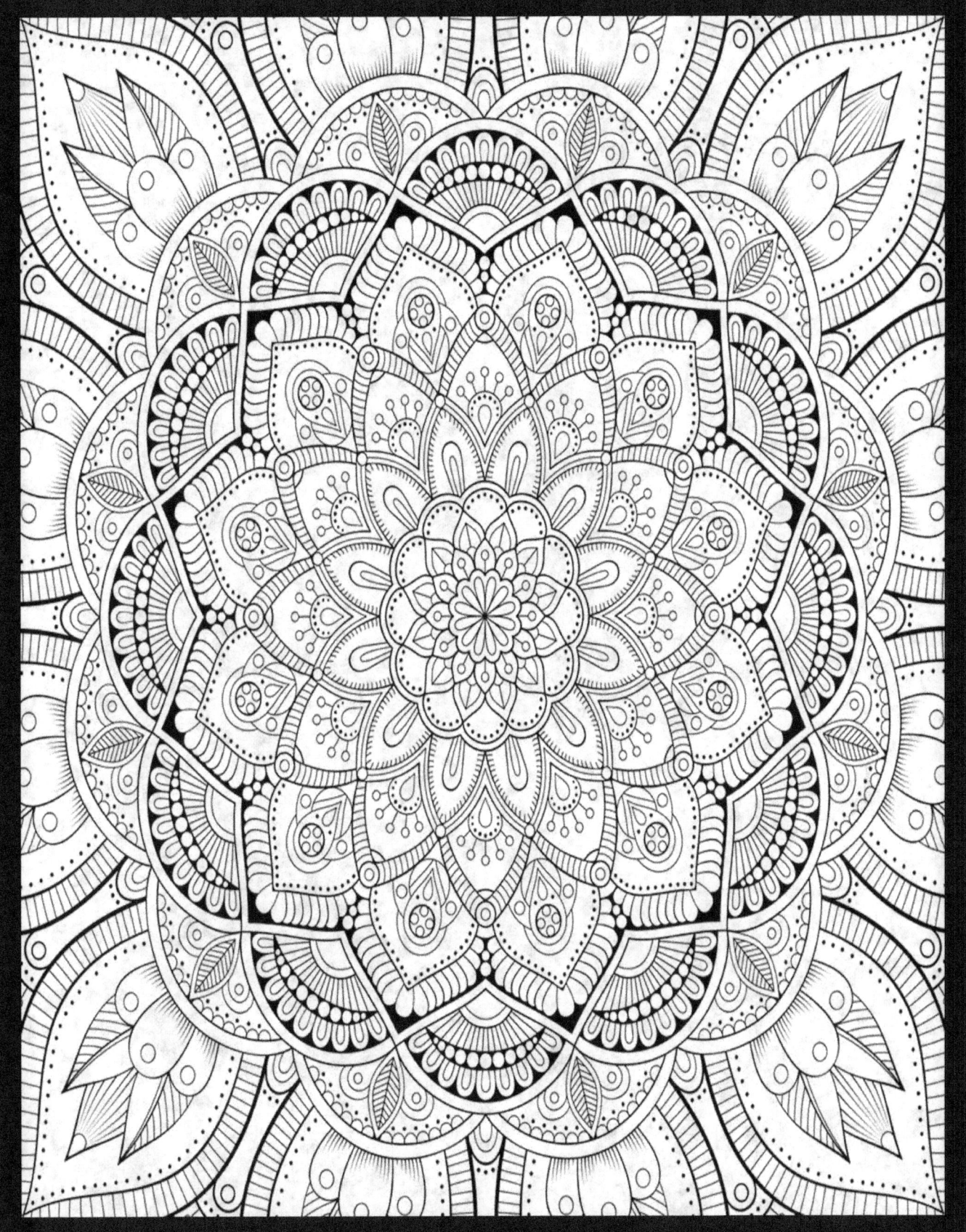

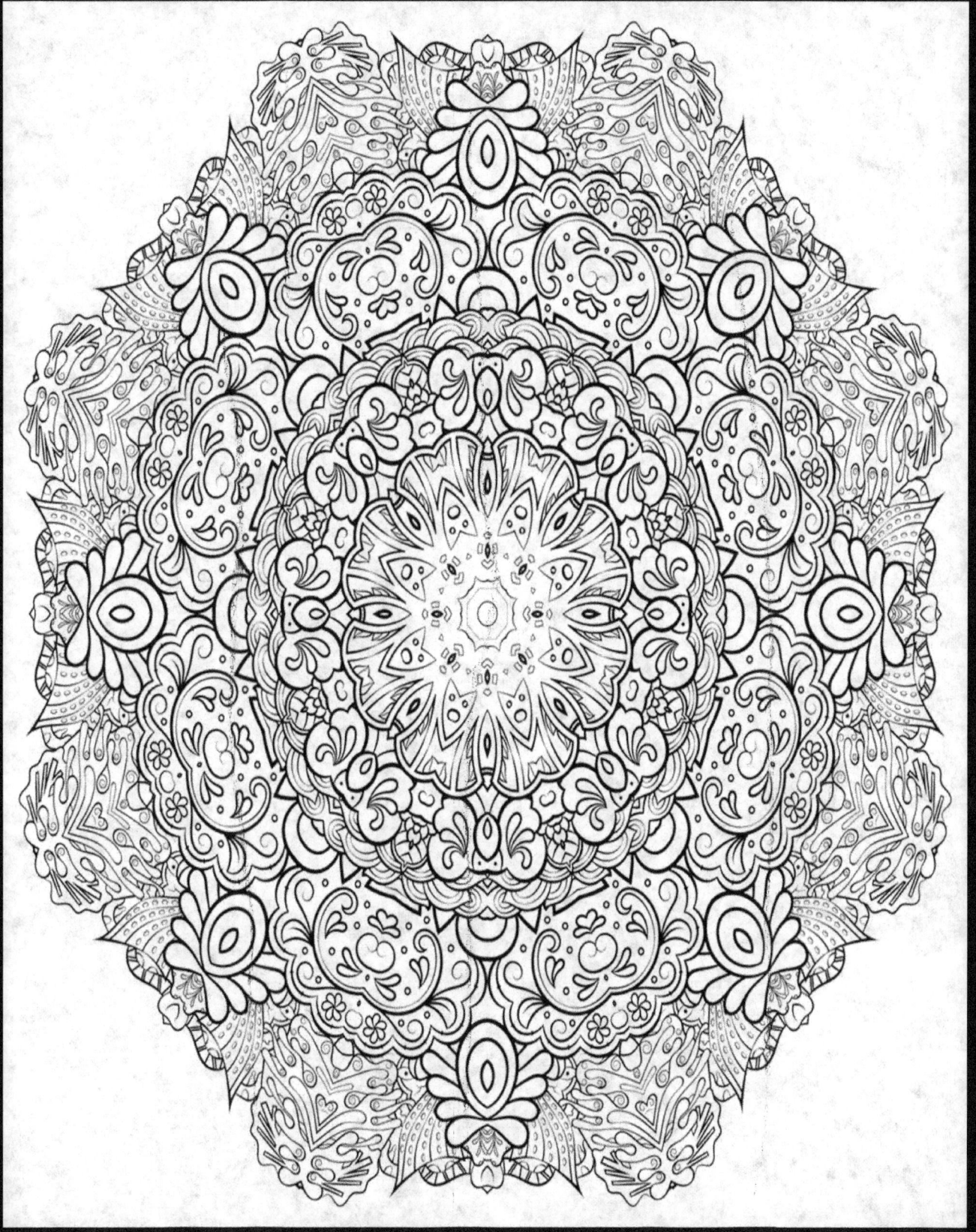

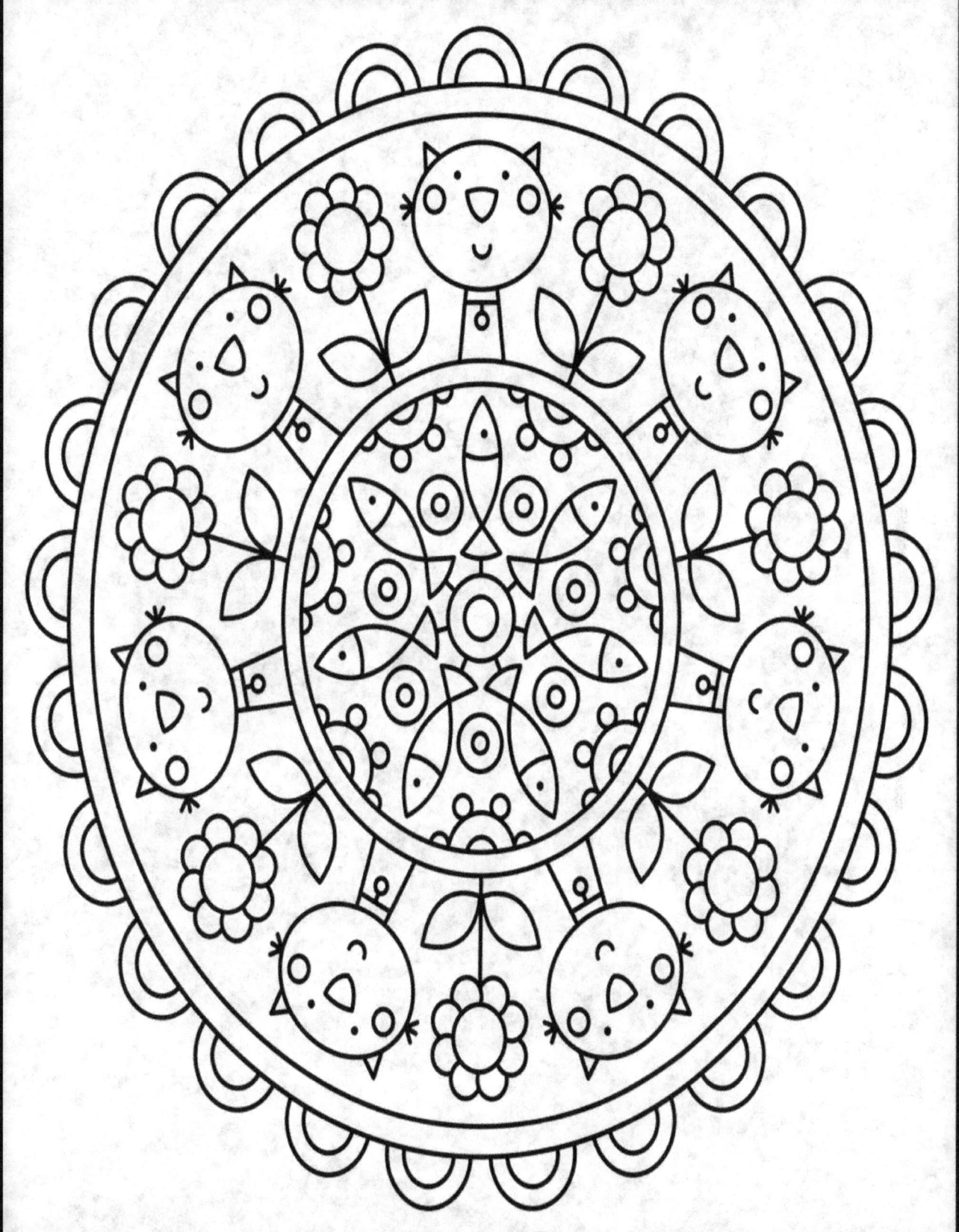

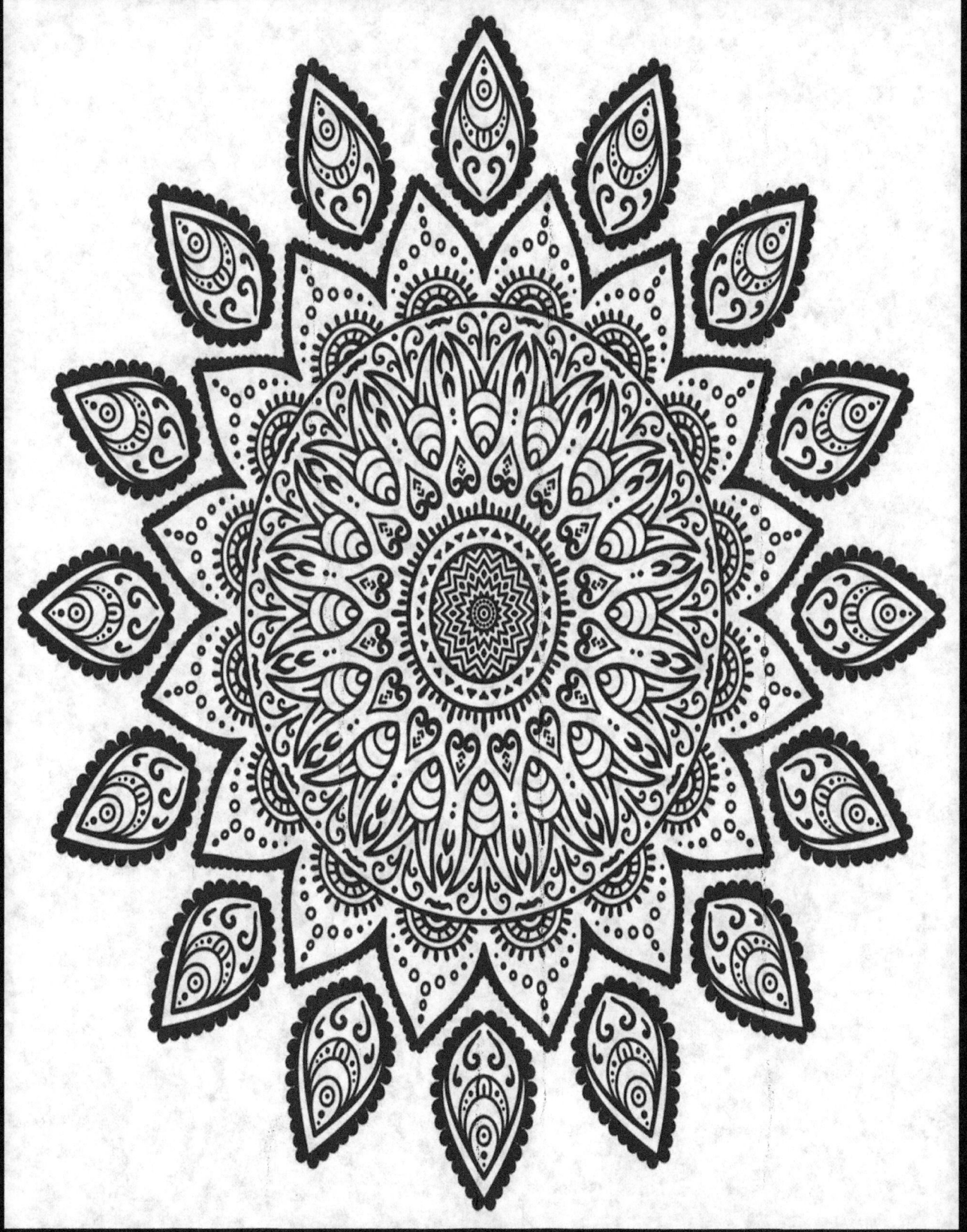

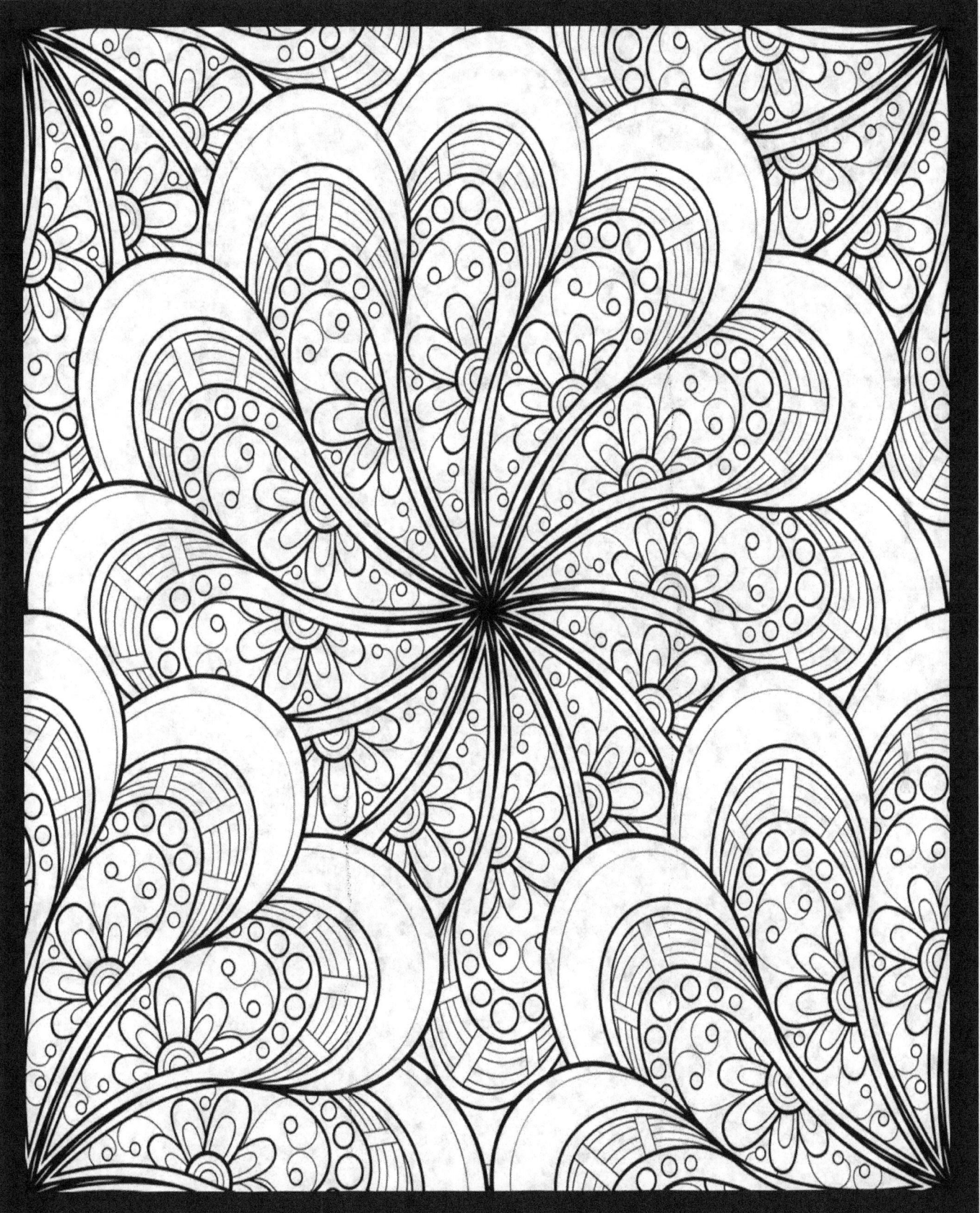

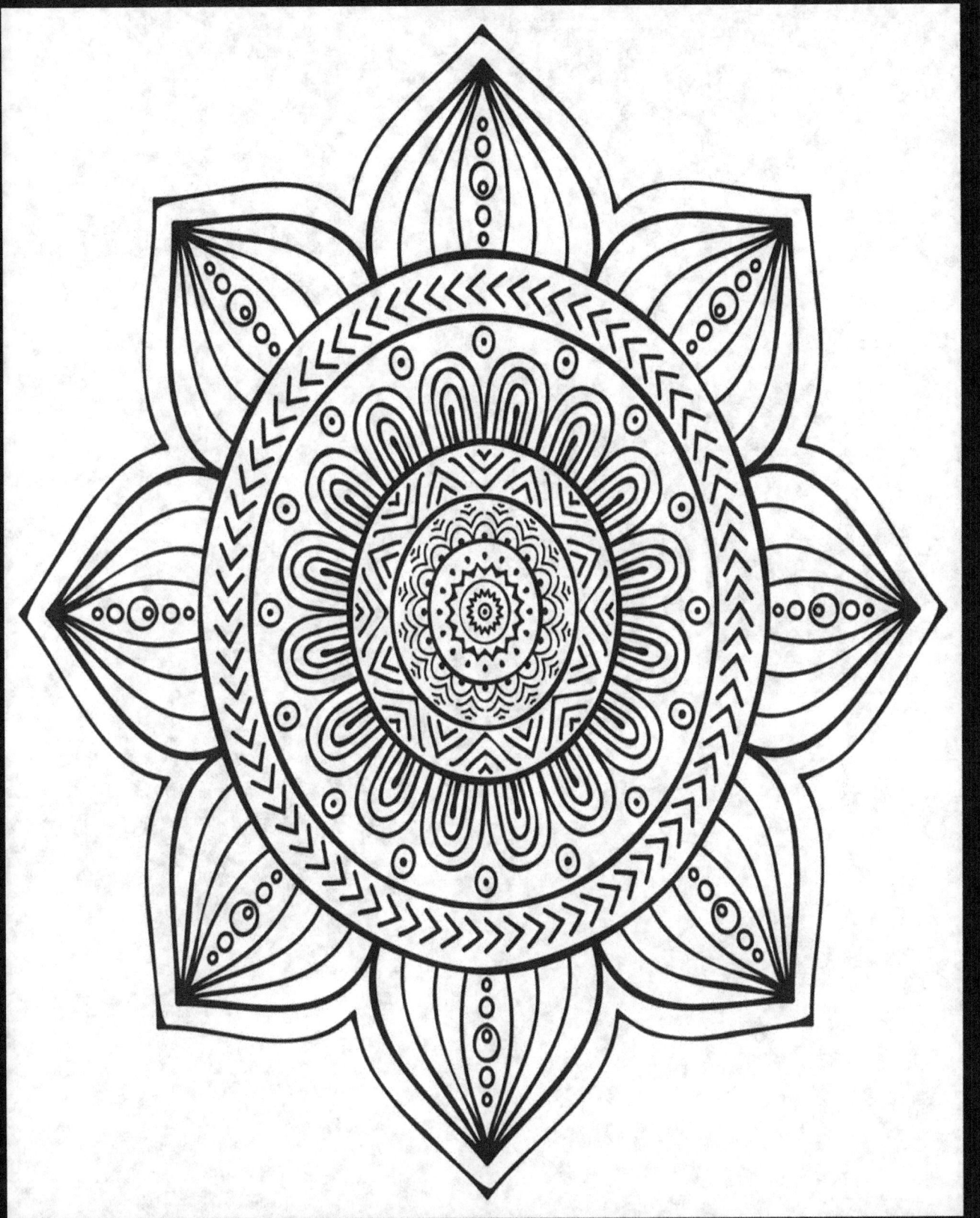

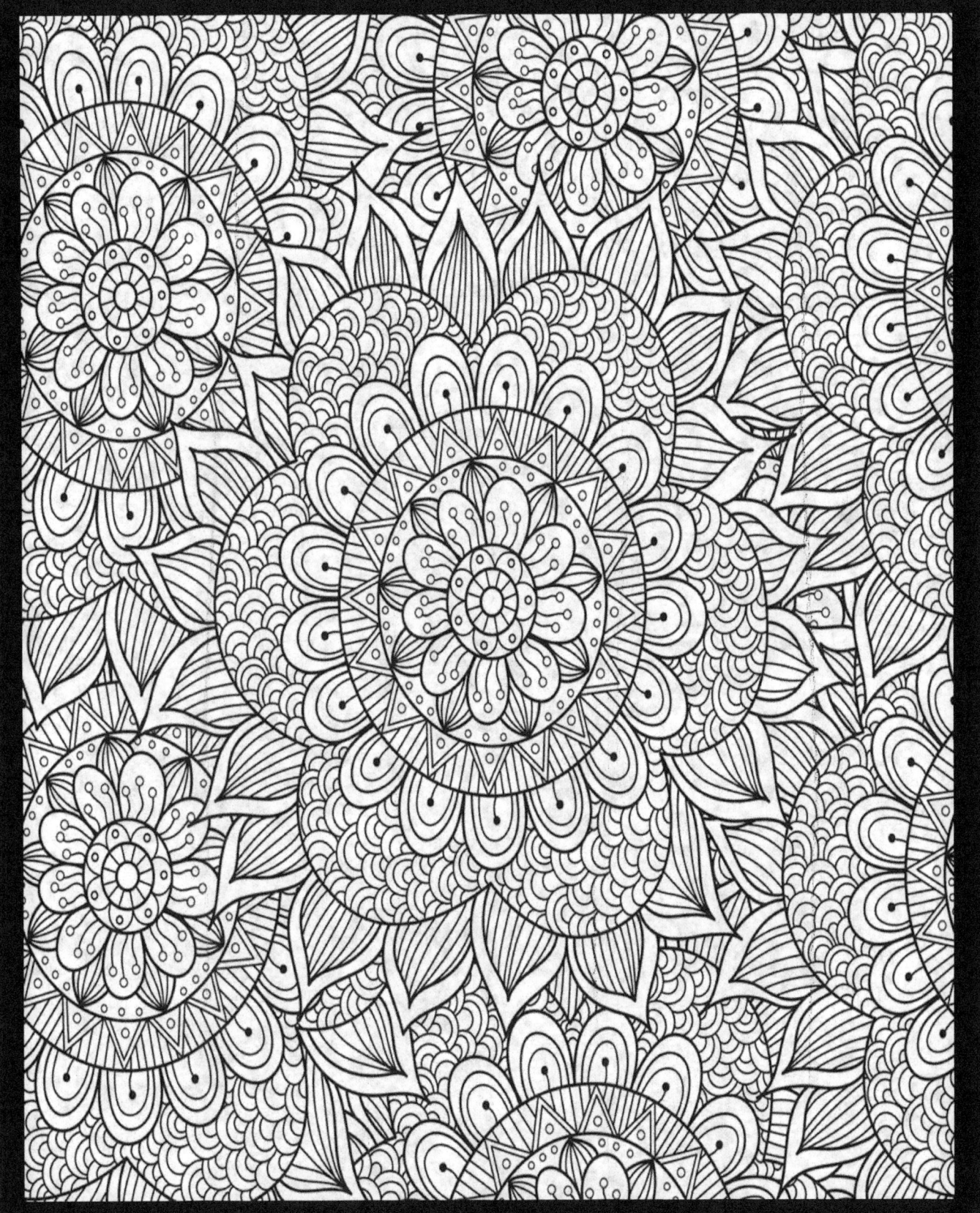

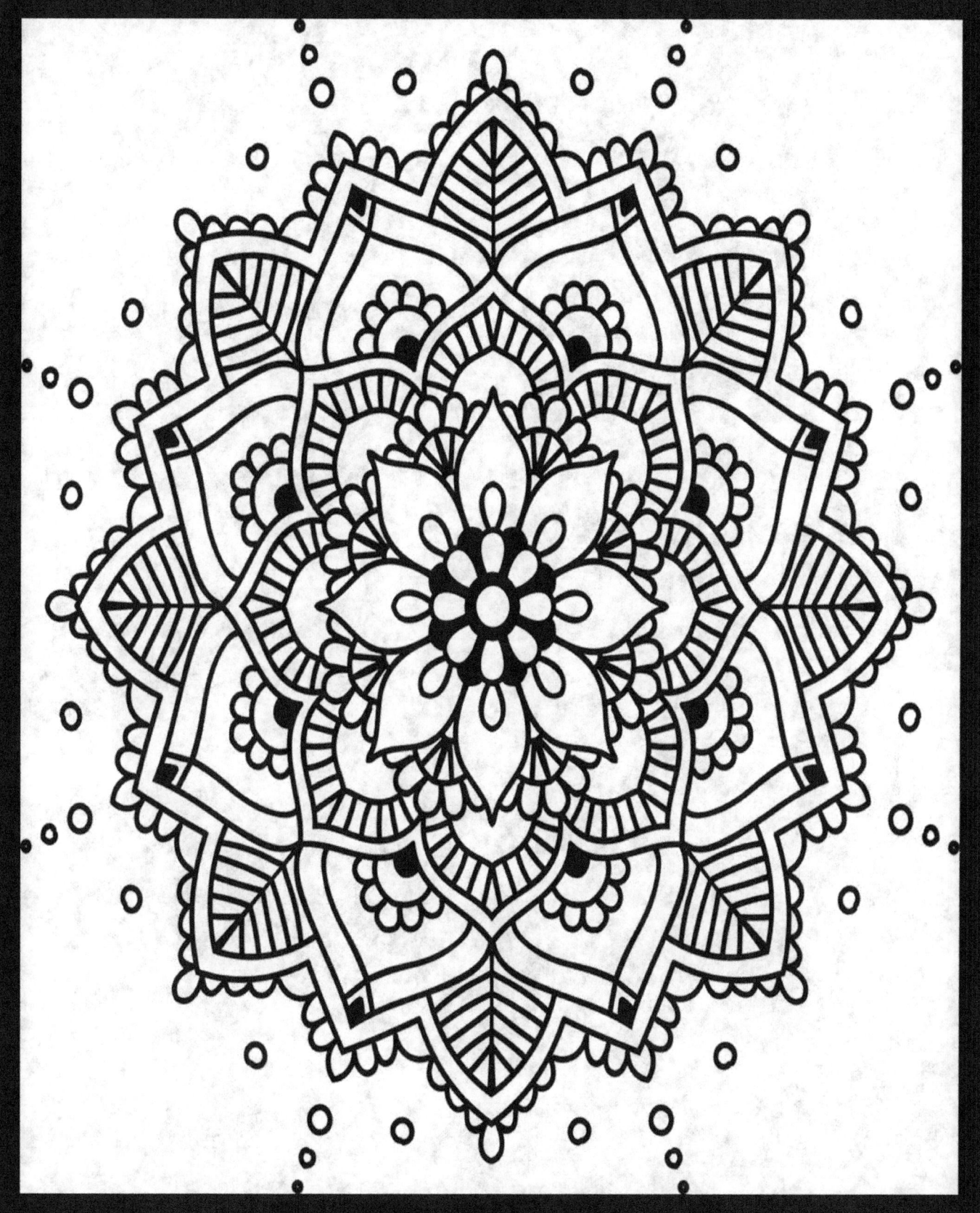

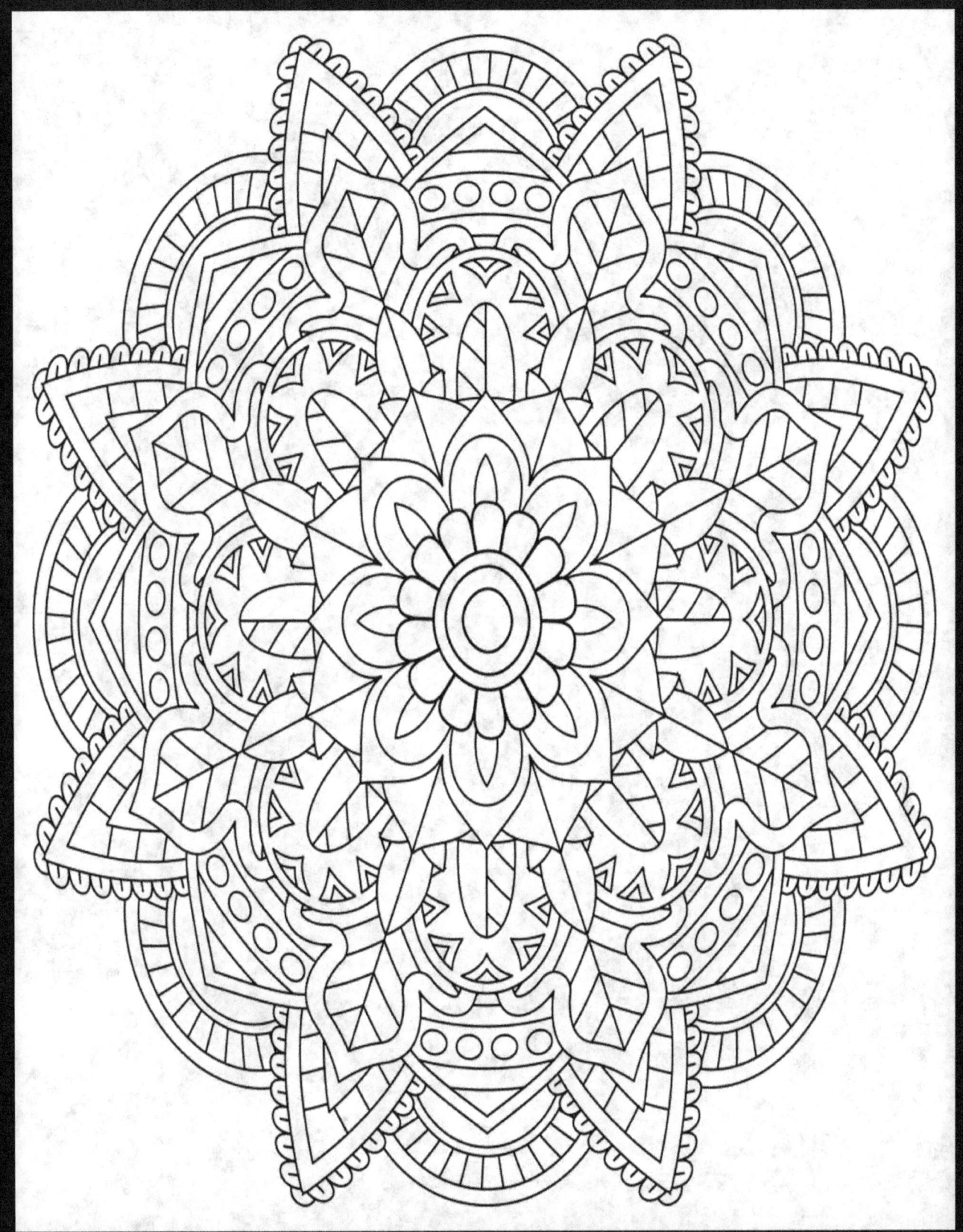

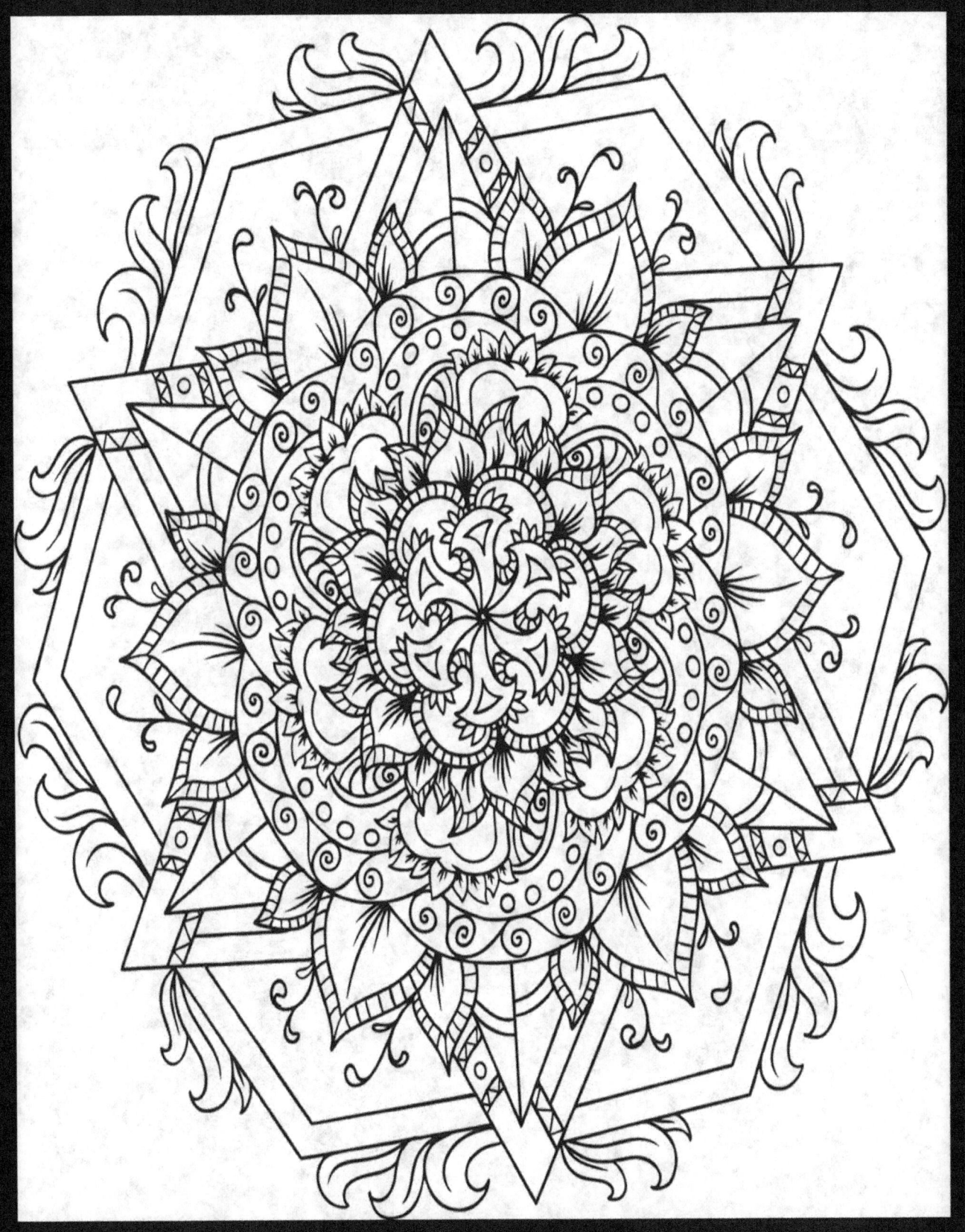

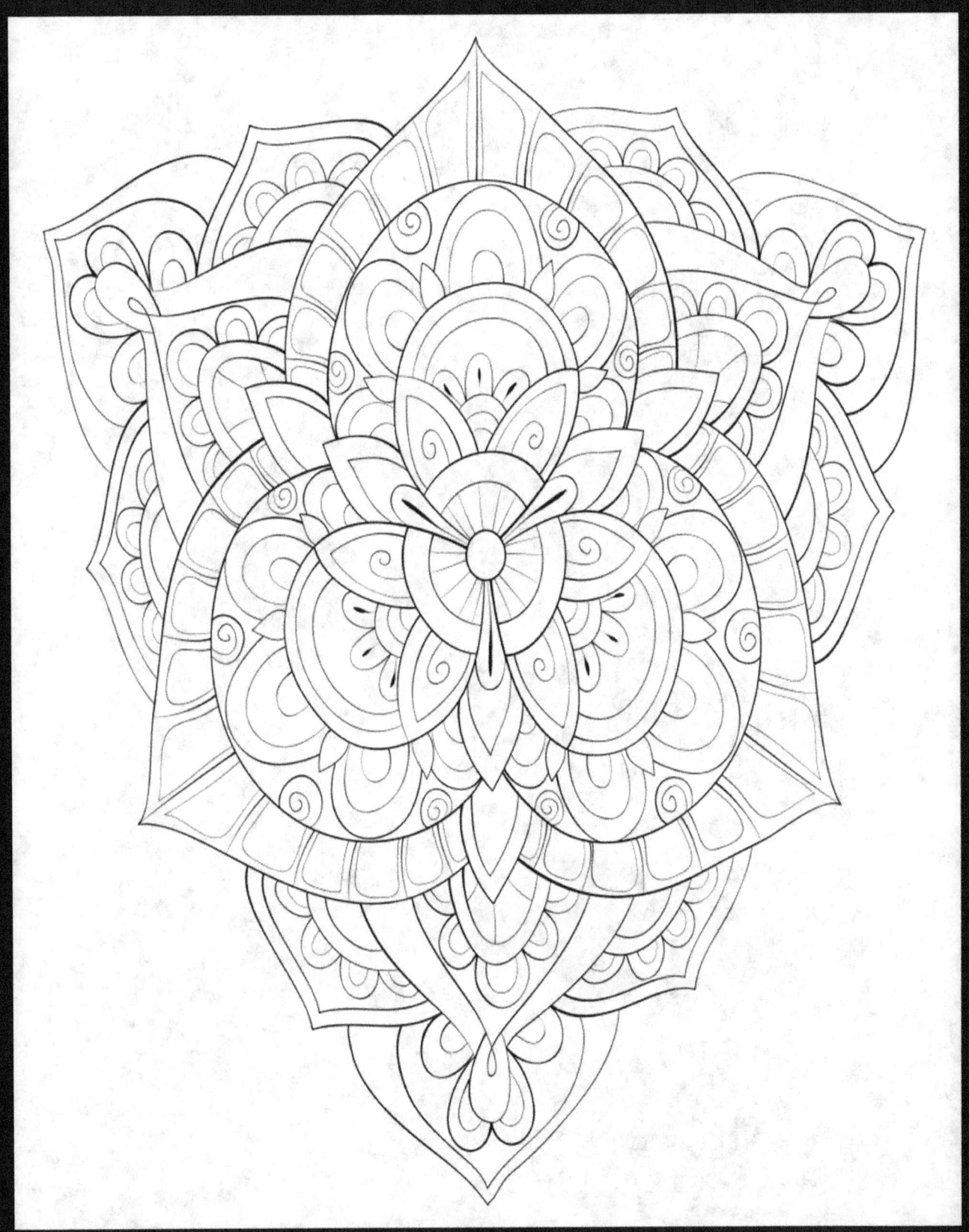

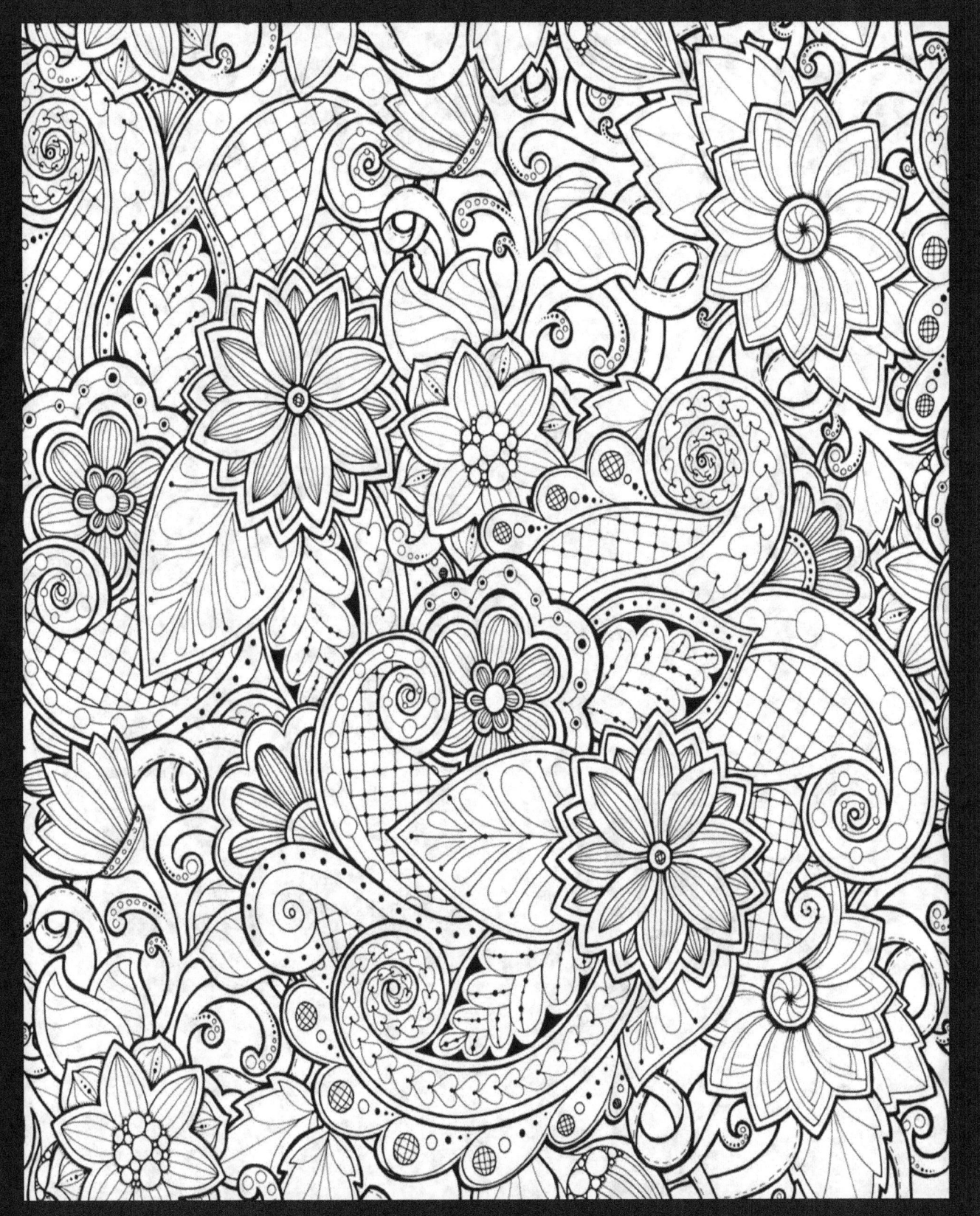

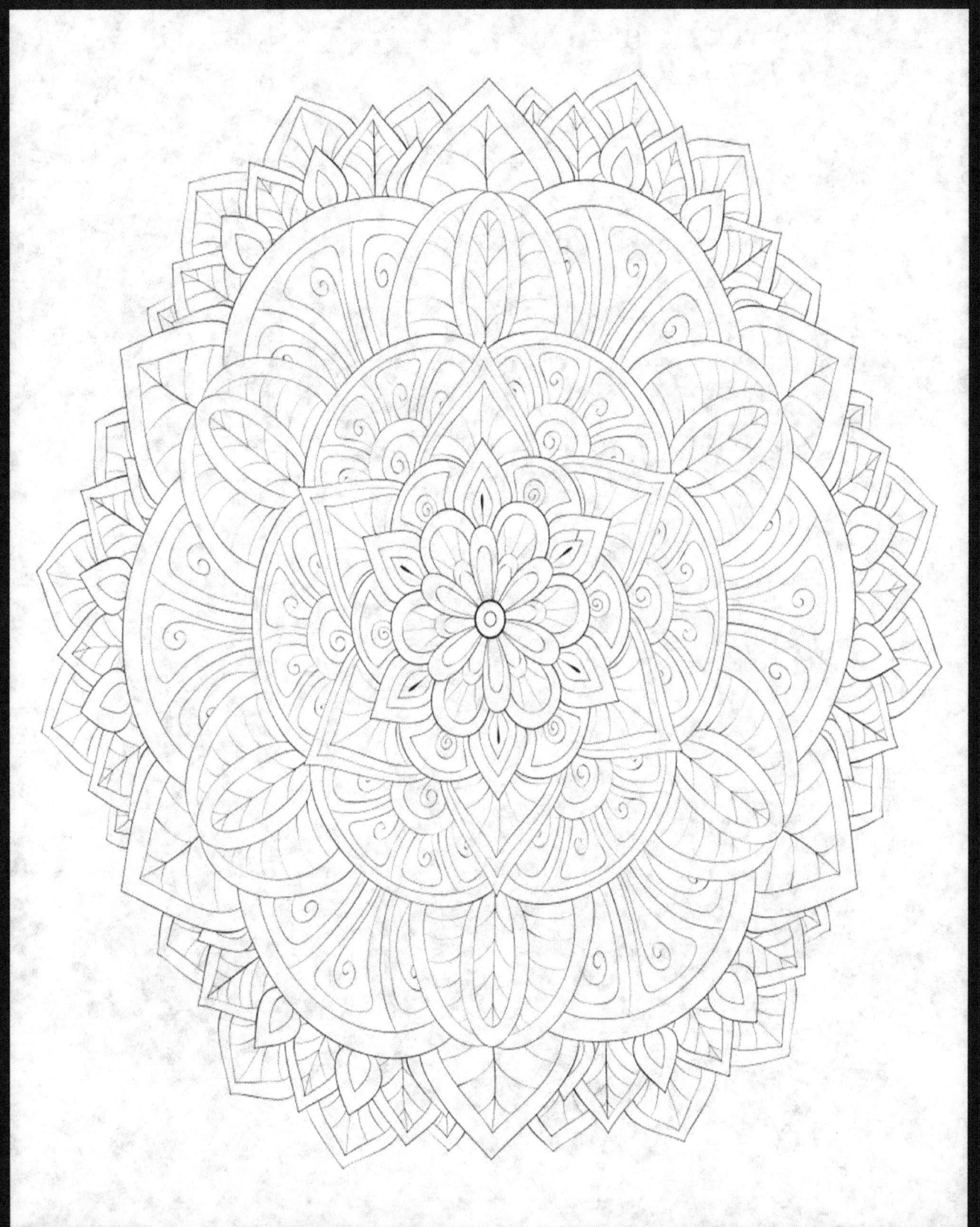

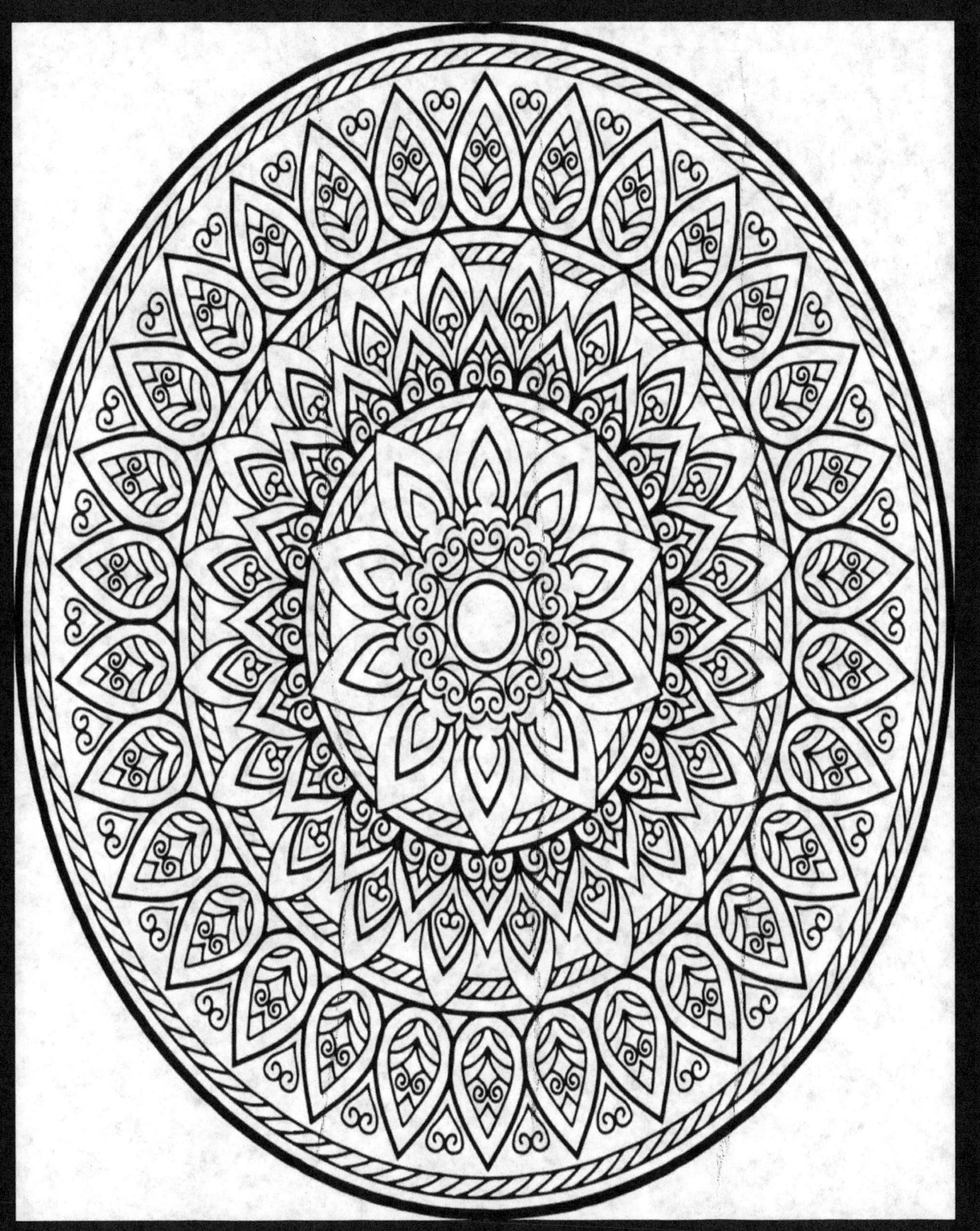

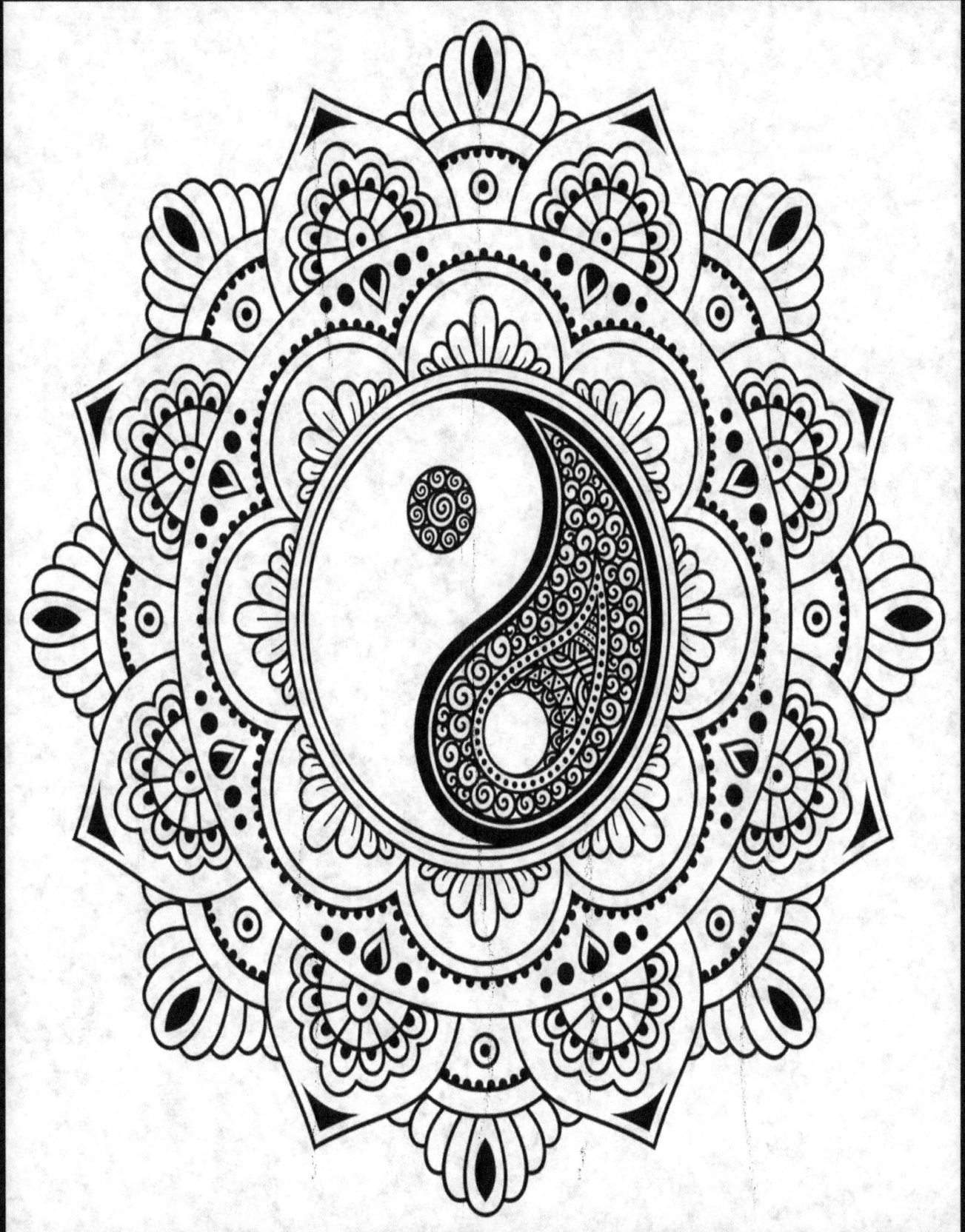

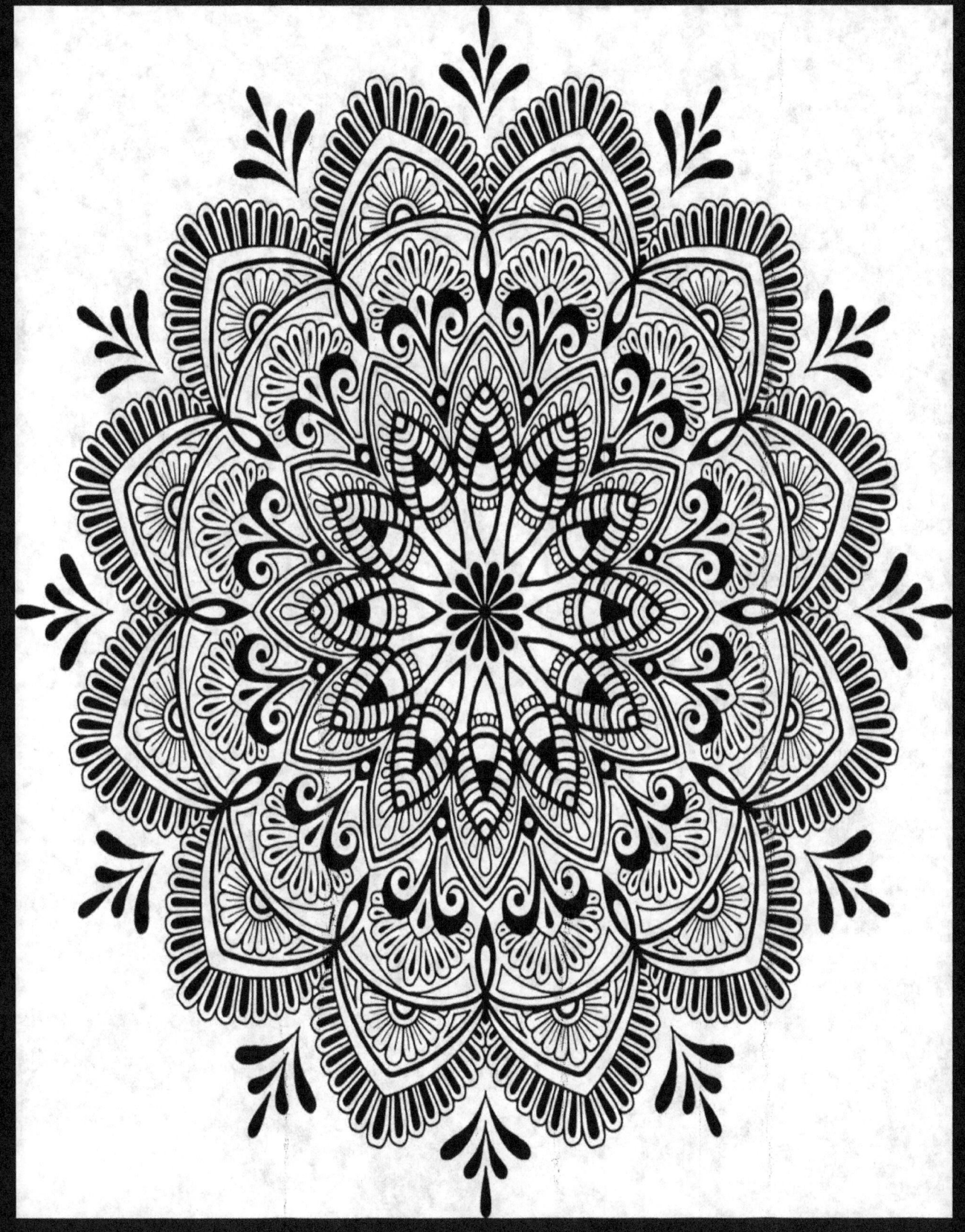

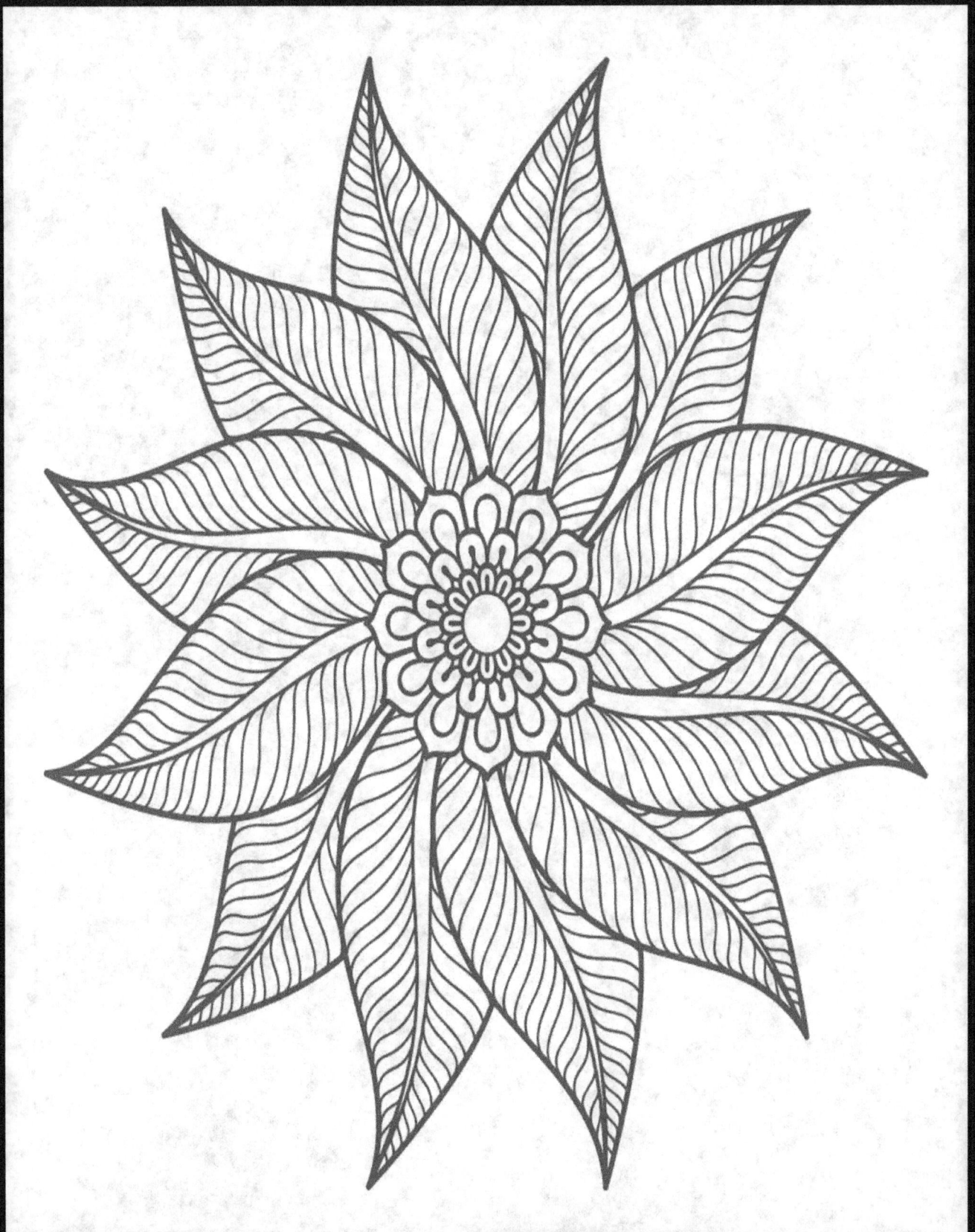

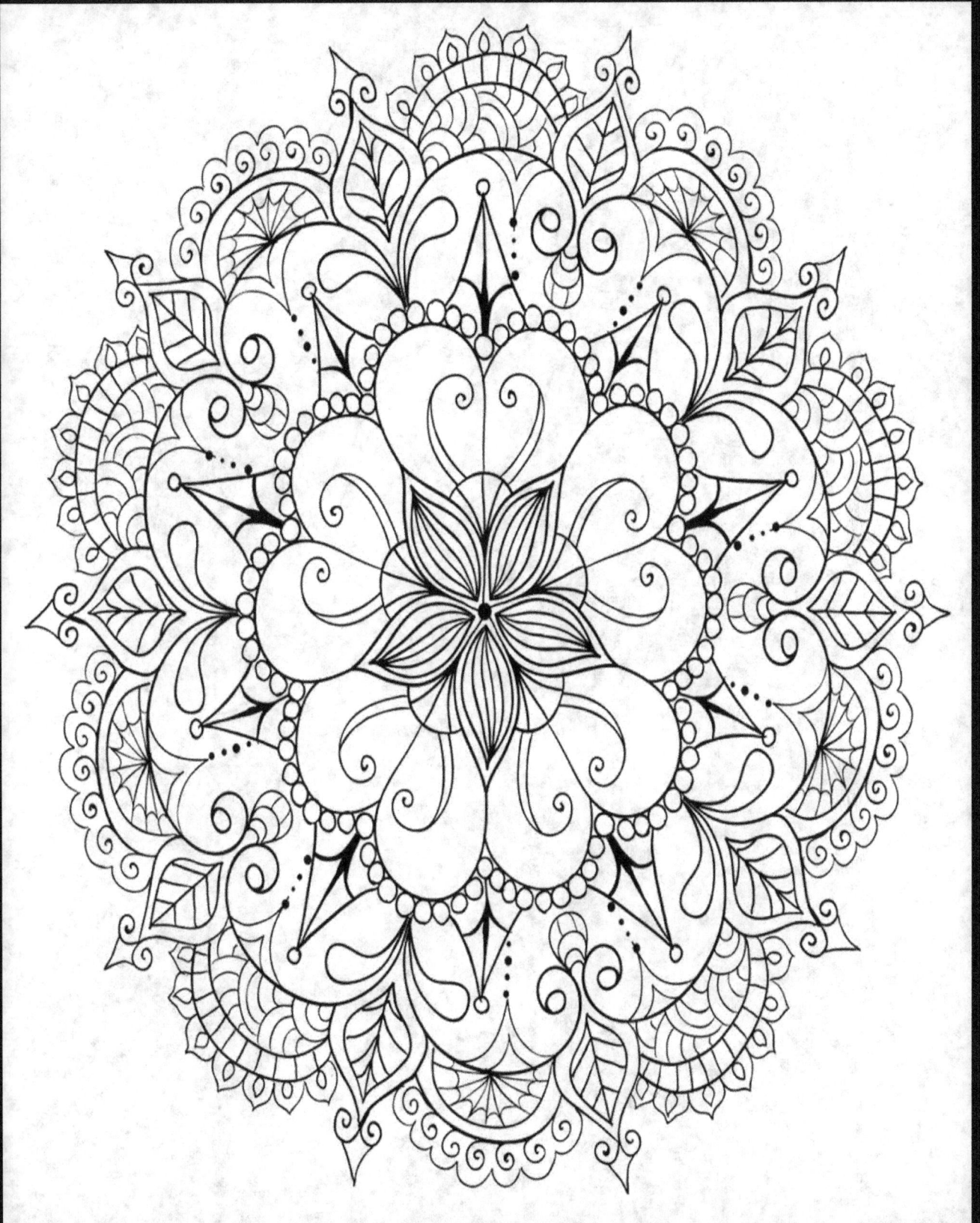

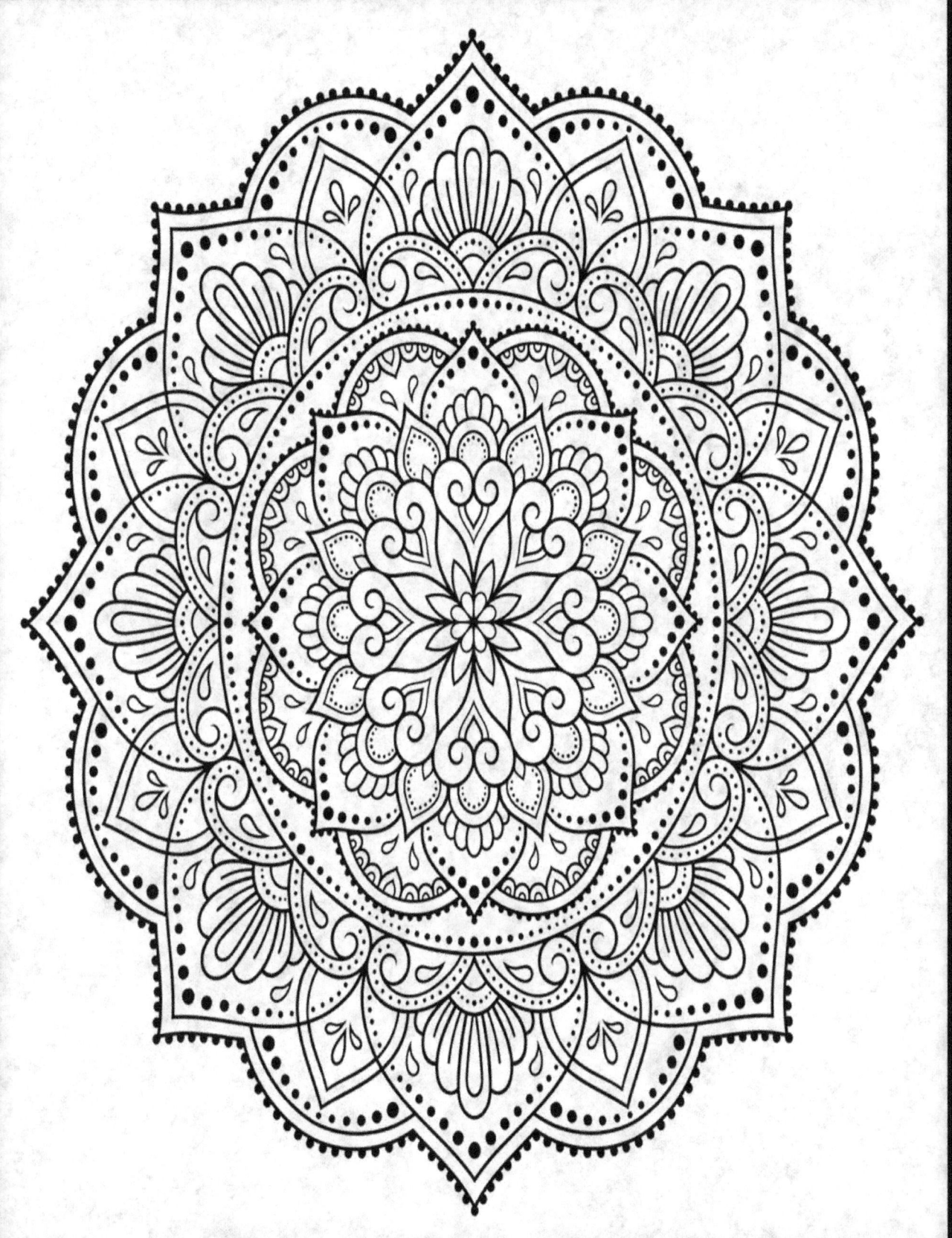

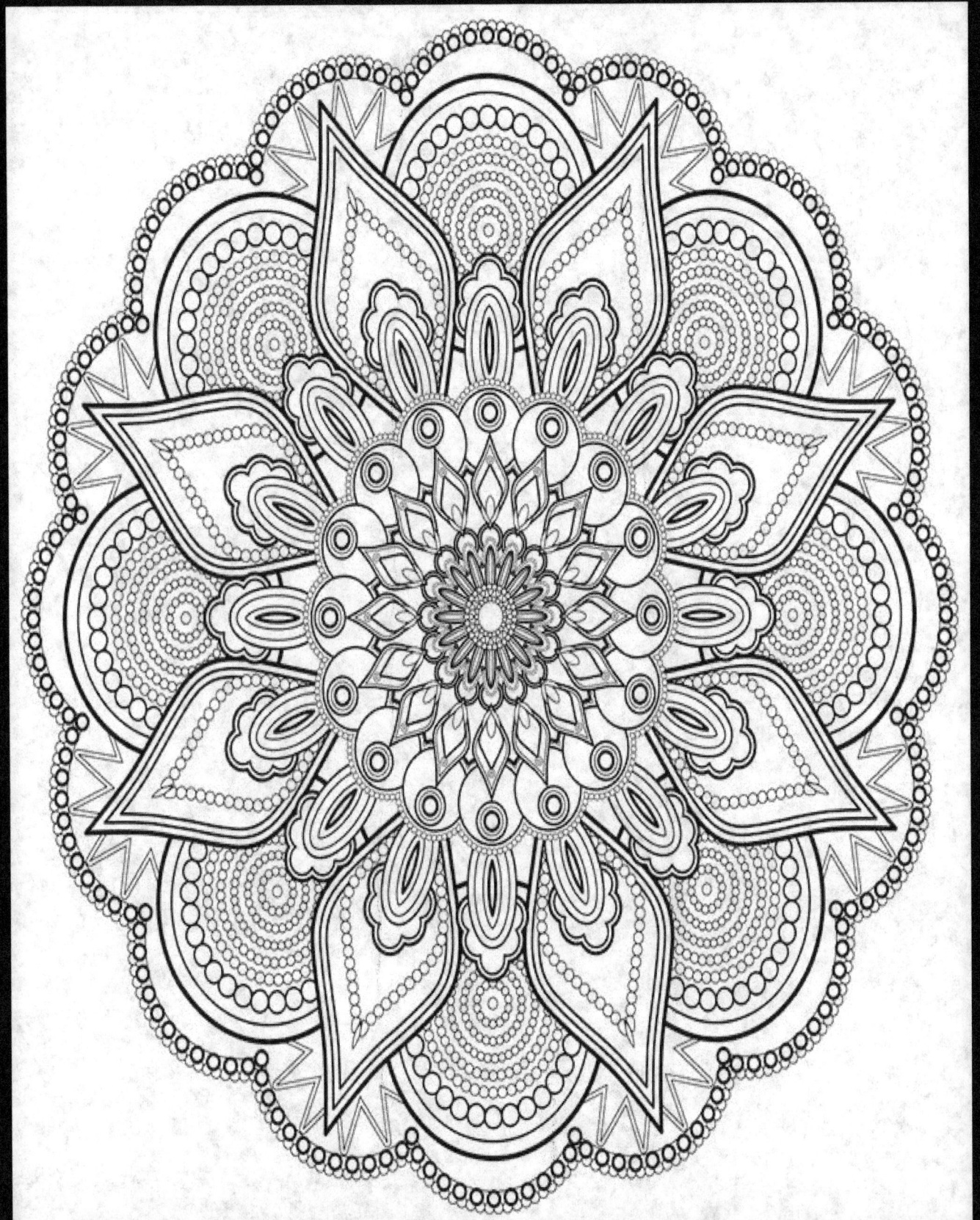

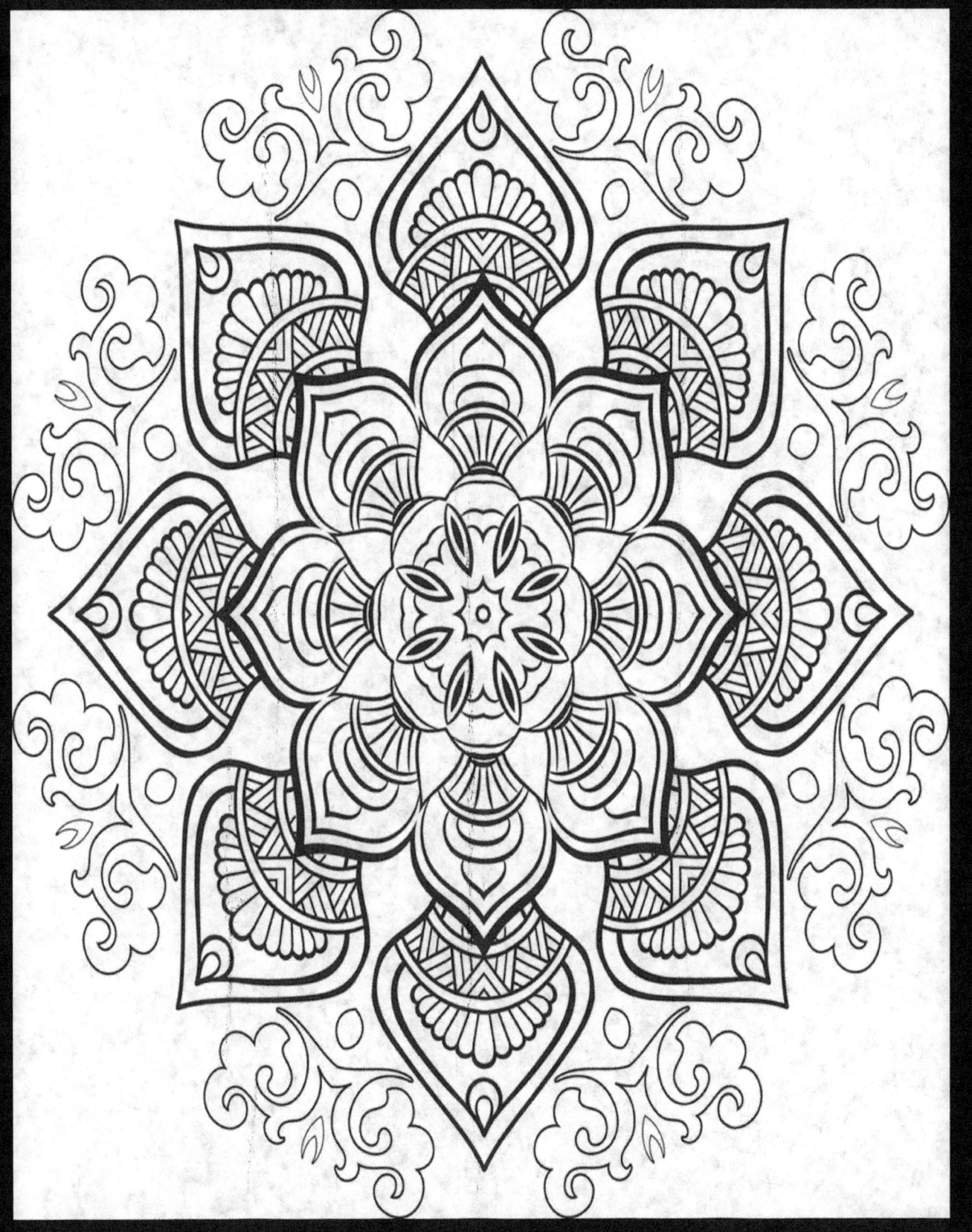

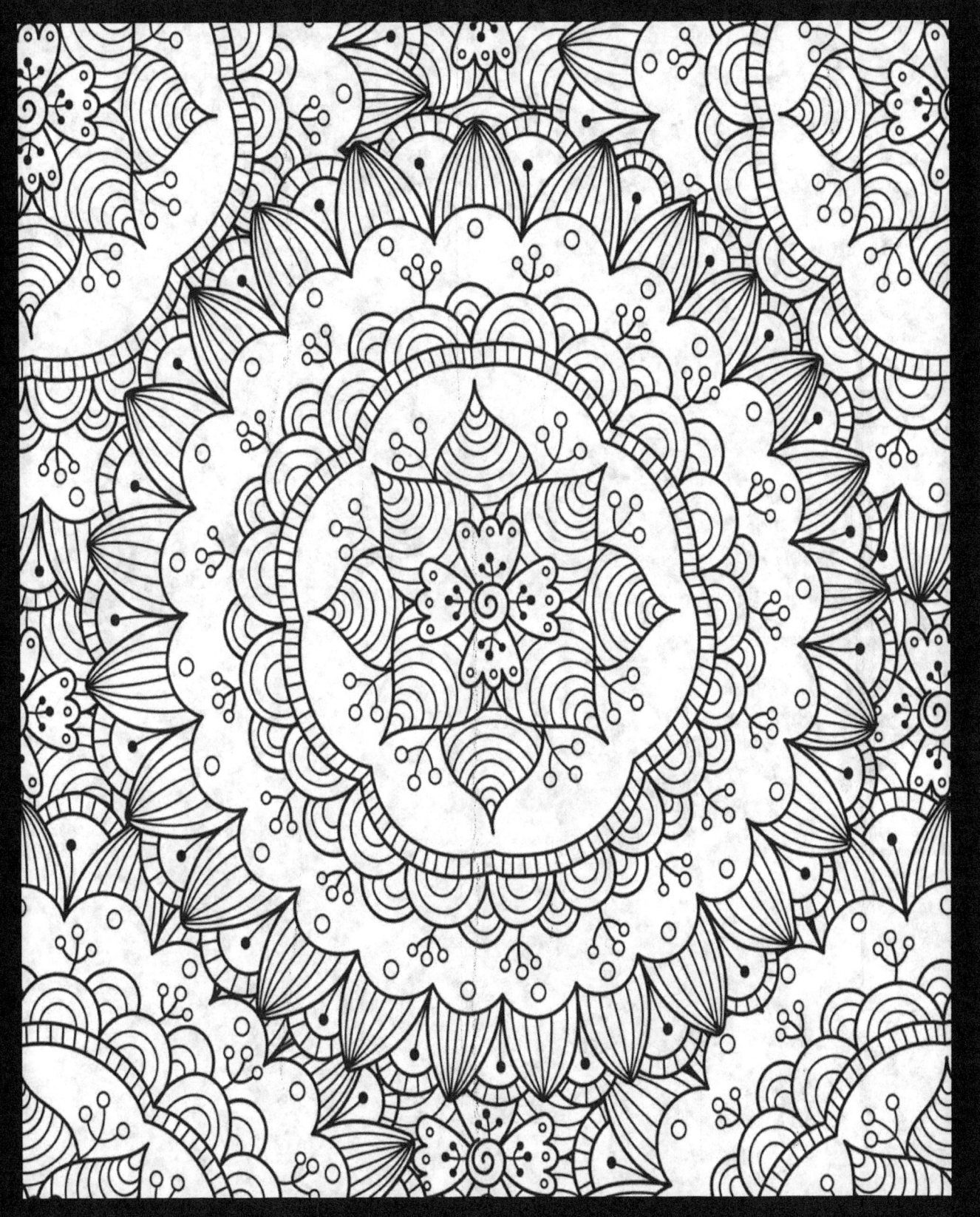

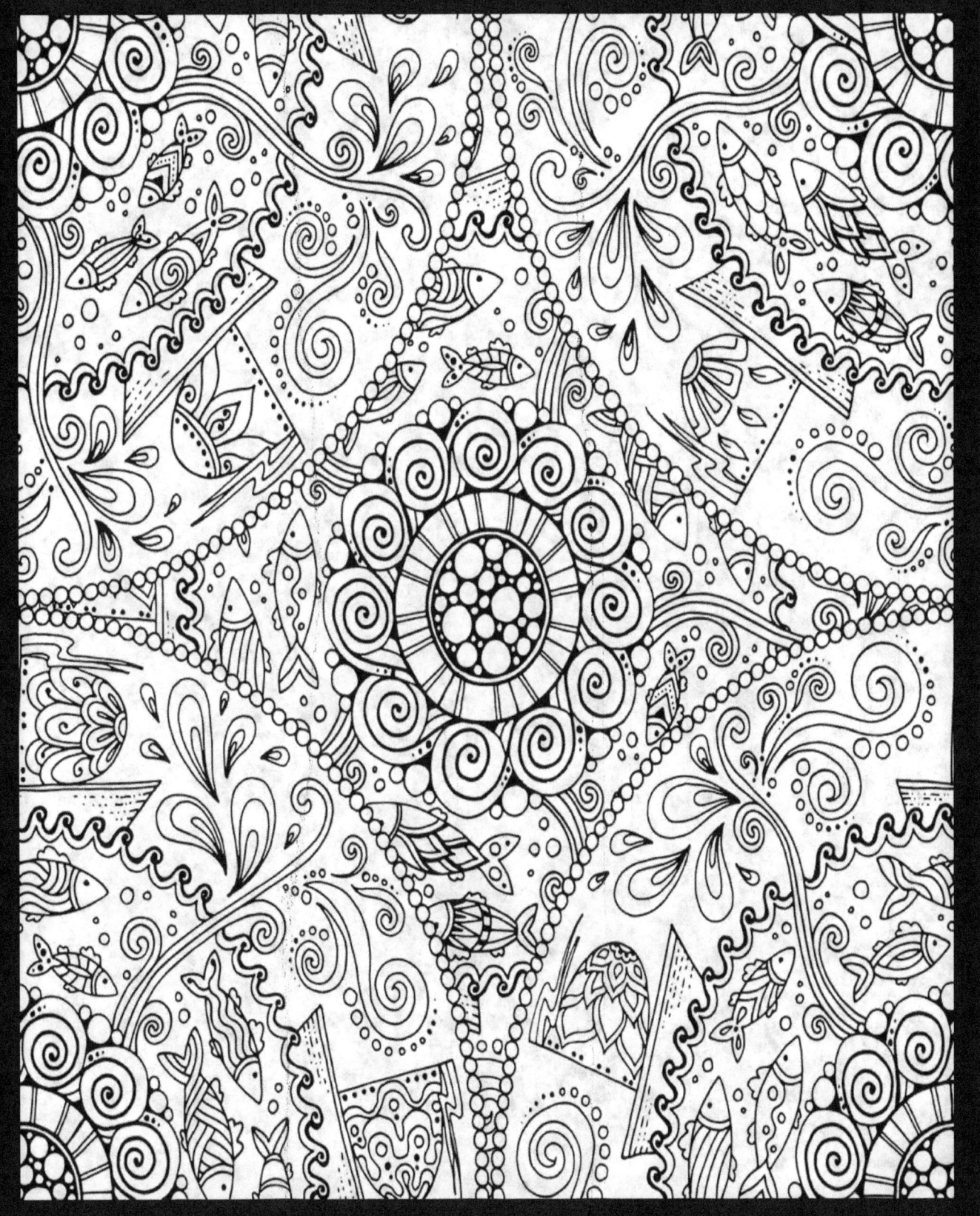

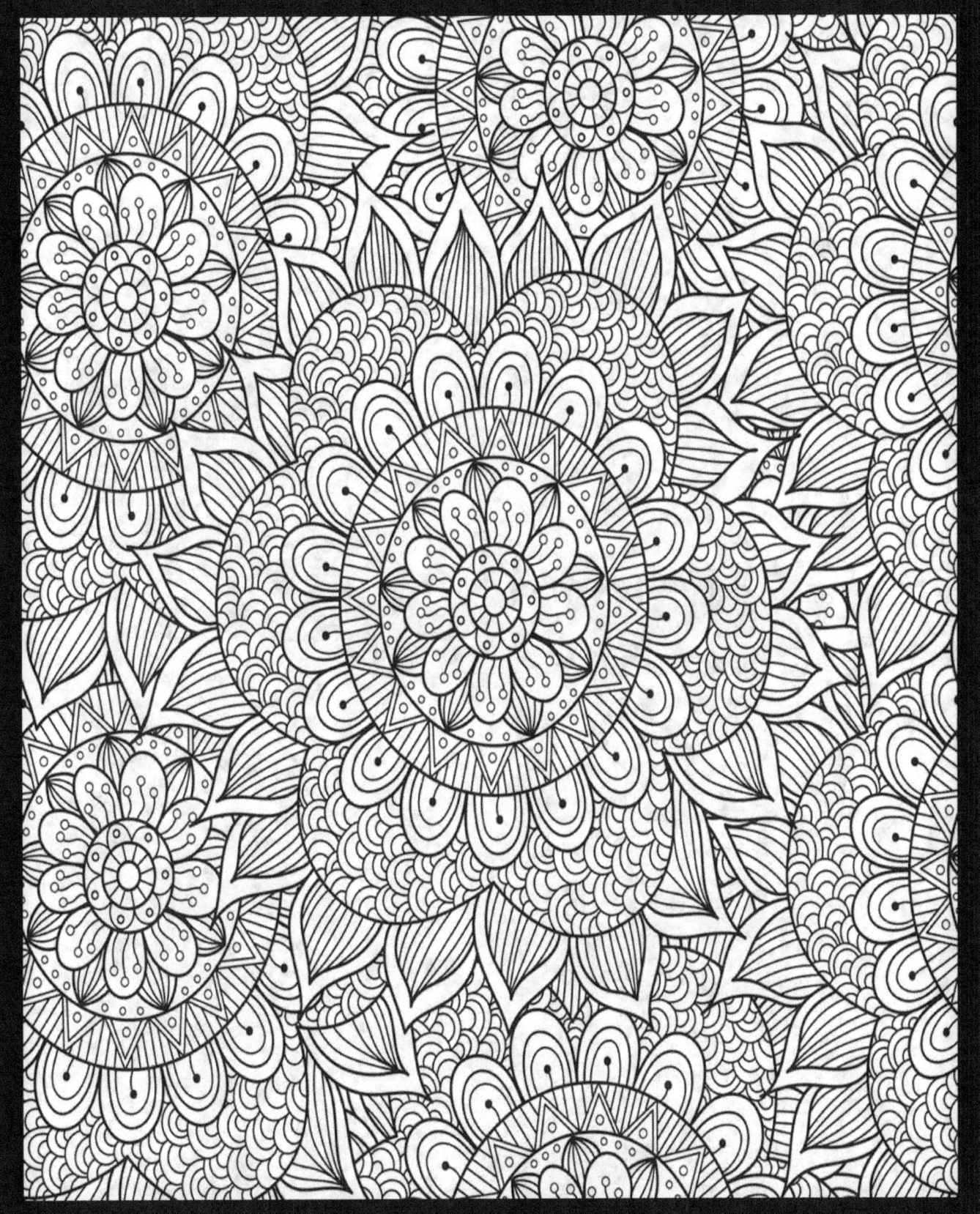

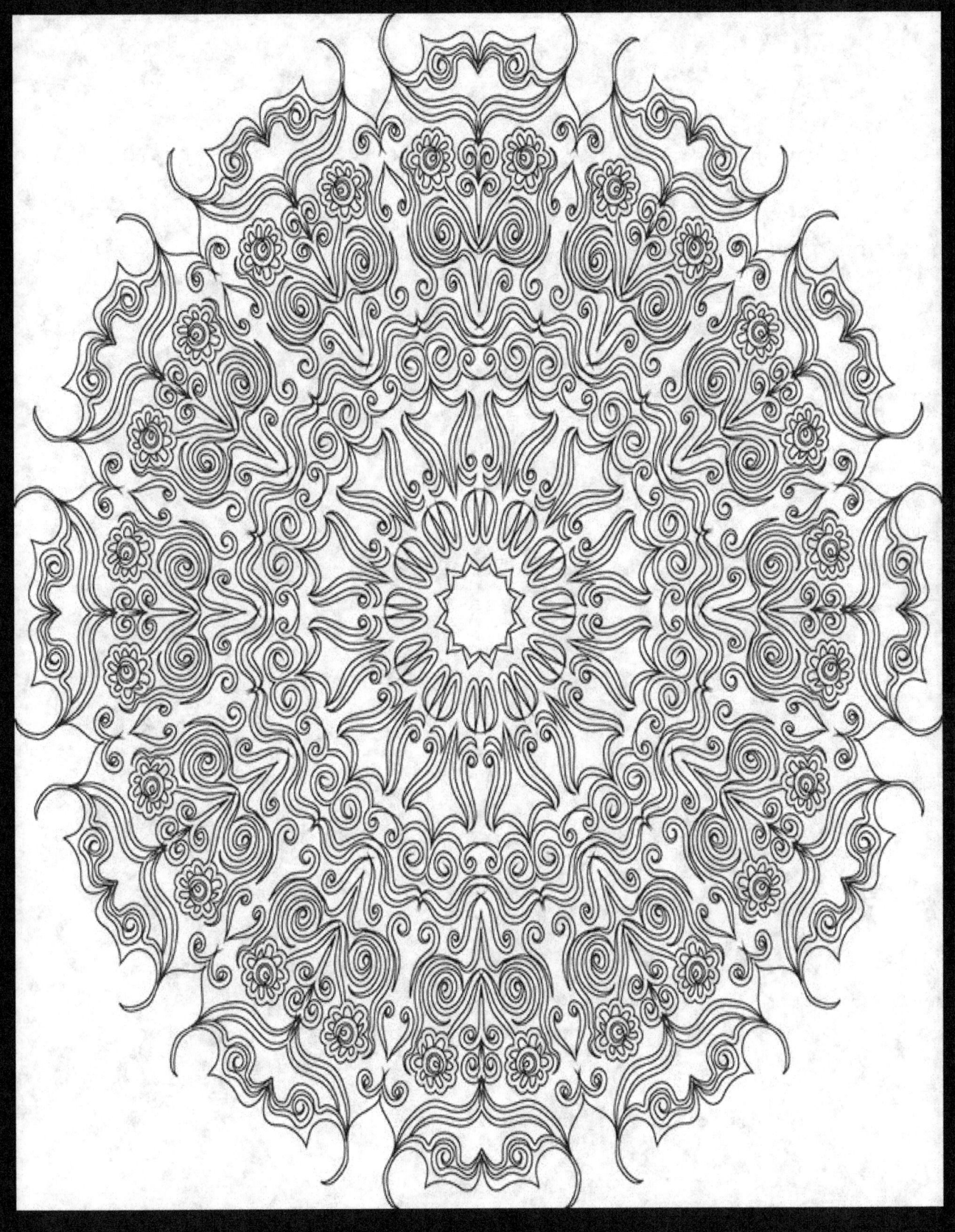

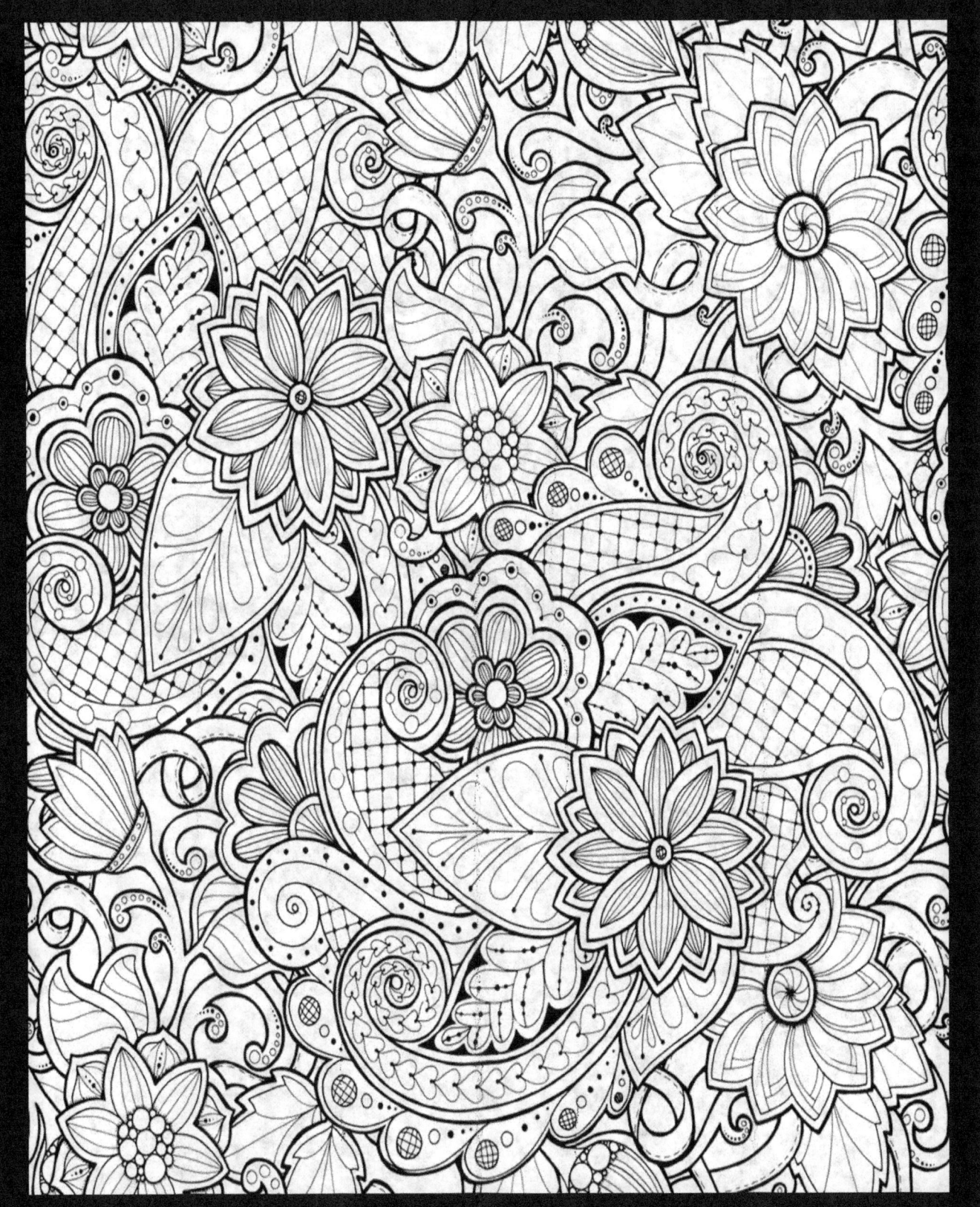

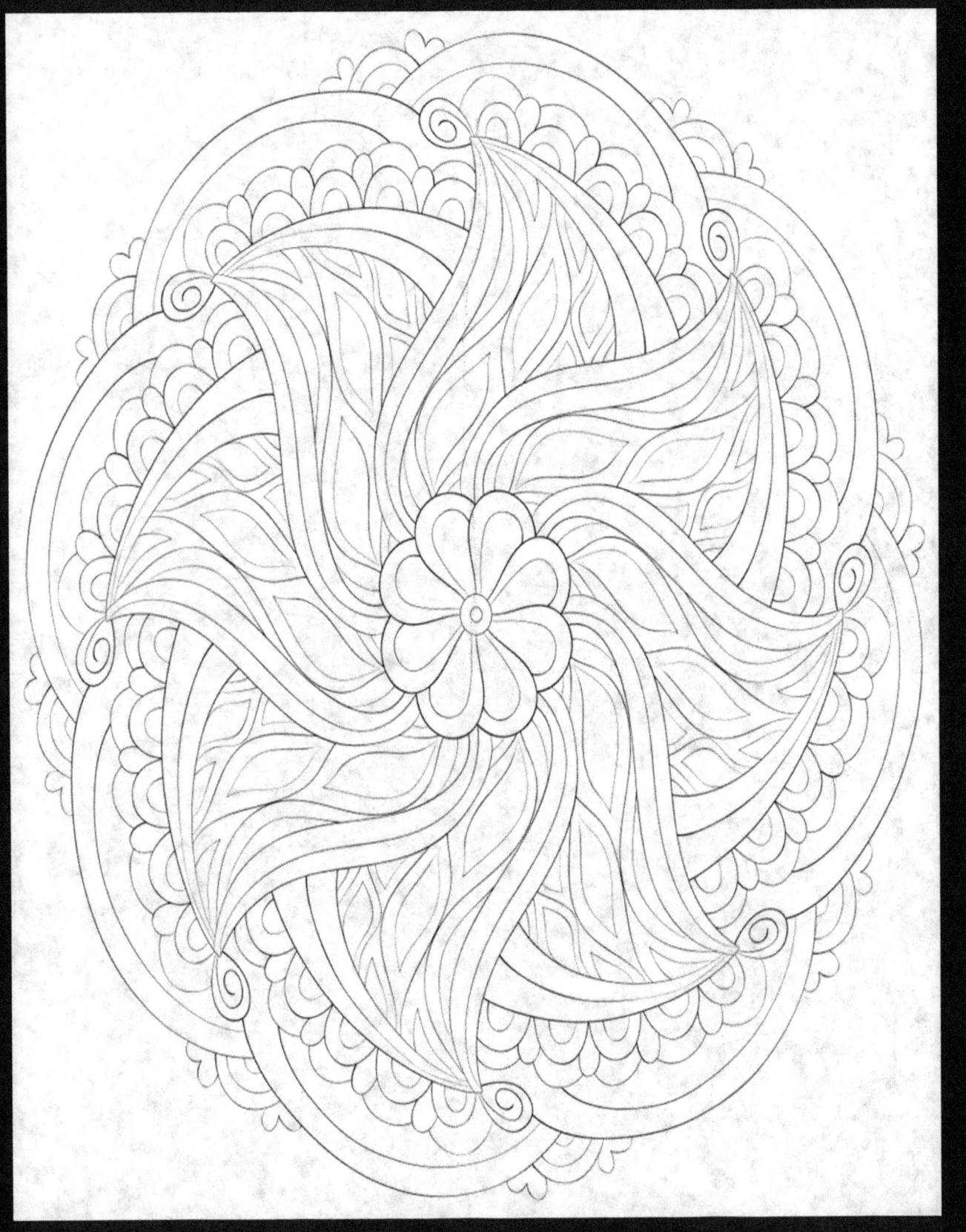

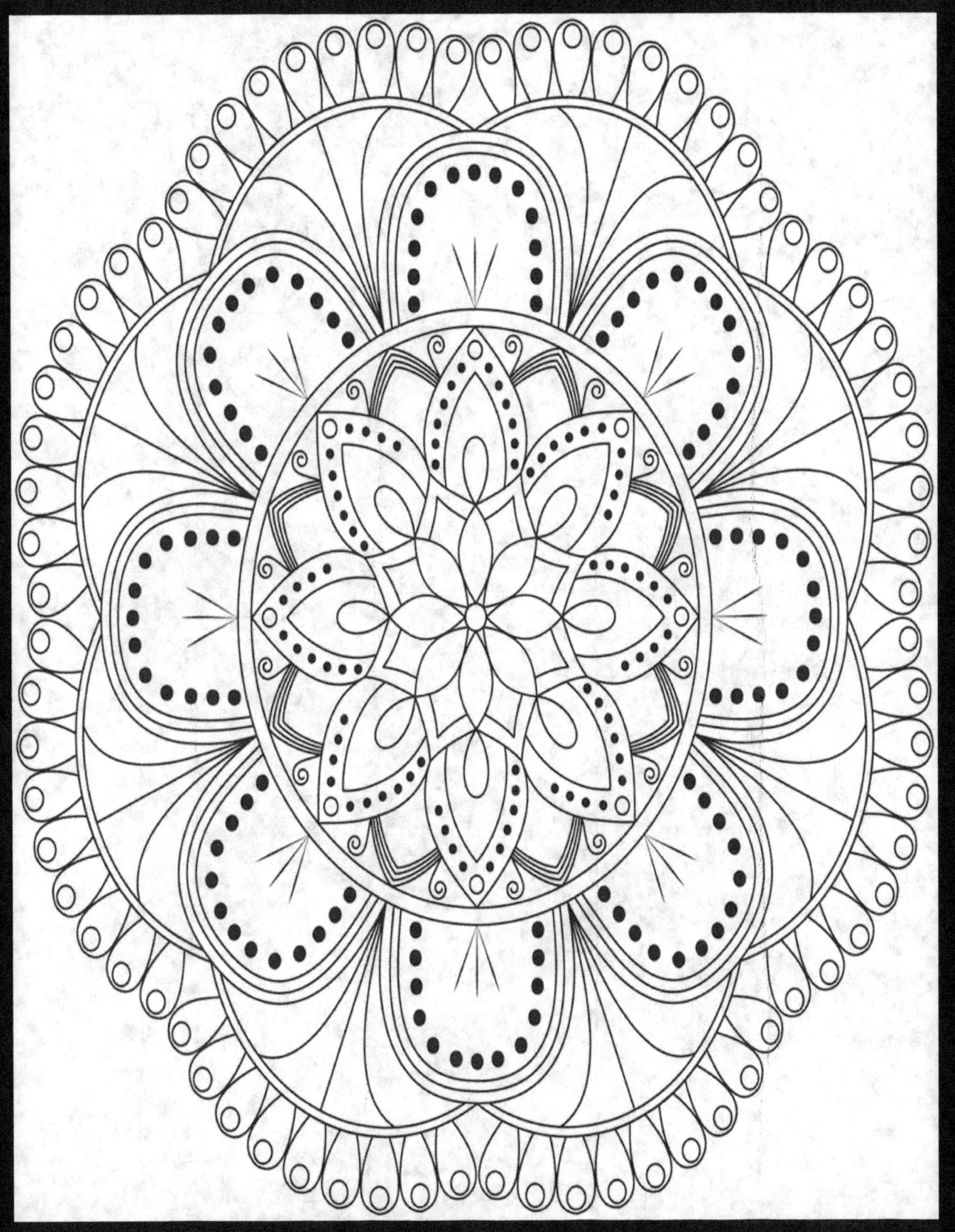

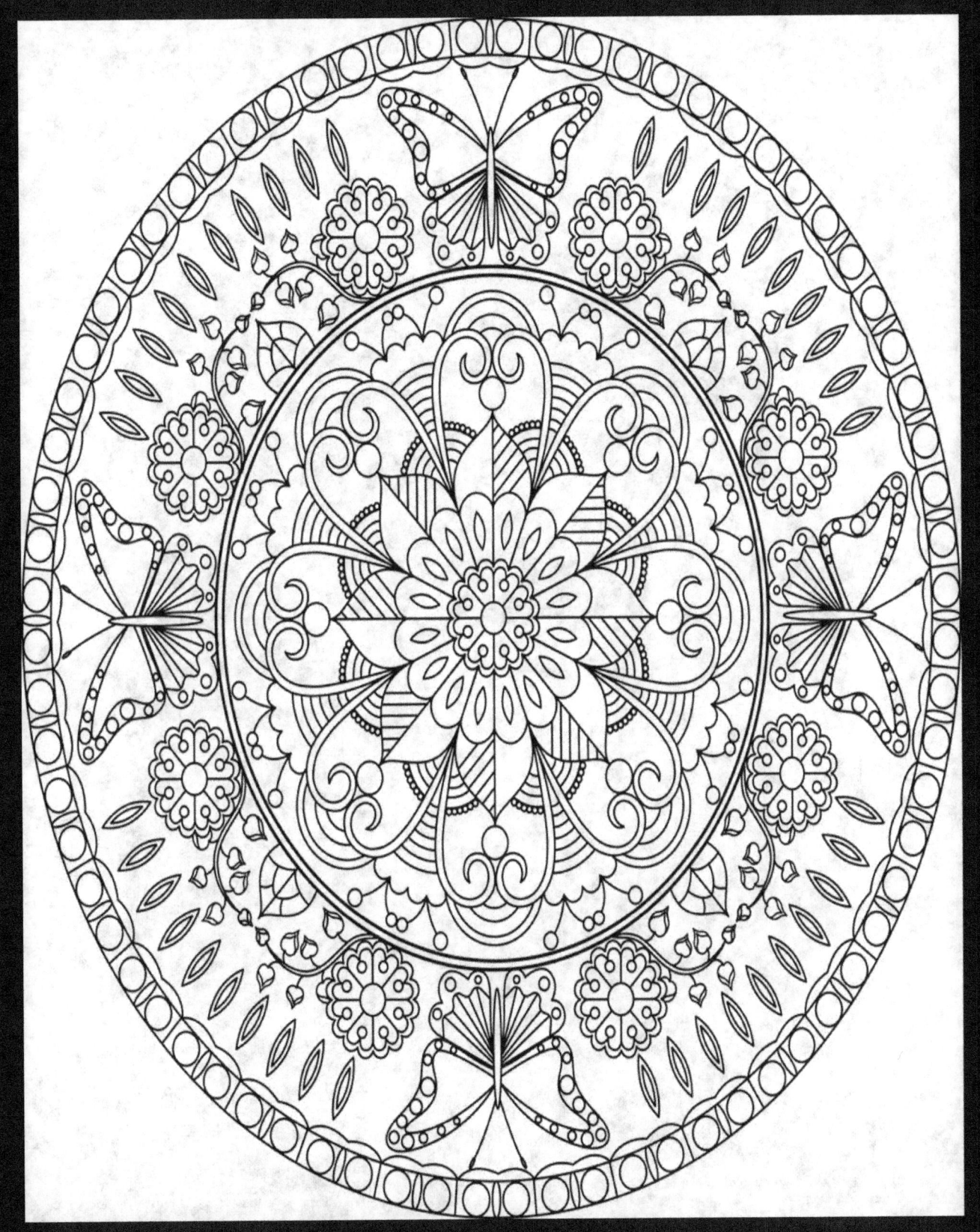

www.ingramcontent.com/pod-product-compliance
Lightning Source LLC
Chambersburg PA
CBHW08045522052026
45465CB00006B/2276